Forecasting the Telephone:
A Retrospective Technology Assessment

COMMUNICATION AND INFORMATION SCIENCE

A series of monographs, treatises, and texts
Edited by
MELVIN J. VOIGT
University of California, San Diego

William C. Adams • Television Coverage of International Affairs
    William C. Adams • Television Coverage of the Middle East
Hewitt D. Crane • The New Social Marketplace: Notes on Effecting Social Change in
    America's Third Century
Rhonda J. Crane • The Politics of International Standards: France and the Color TV War
Glen Fisher • American Communicatipn in a Global Society
Oscar H. Gandy, Jr. • Beyond Agenda Setting: Information Subsidies and Public Policy
Edmund Glenn • Man and Mankind: Conflict and Communication Betwen Cultures
Bradley S. Greenberg • Life on Television: Content Analyses of U.S. TV Drama
Cees J. Hamelink • Finance and Information: A Study of Converging Interests
Robert M. Landau, James H. Bair, and Jean Siegman • Emerging Office Systems
John S. Lawrence and Bernard M. Timberg • Fair Use and Free Inquiry: Copyright Law and
    the New Media
Robert G. Meadow • Politics as Communication
William H. Melody, Liora R. Salter, and Paul Heyer • Culture, Communication, and
    Dependency: The Tradition of H.A. Innis
Vincent Mosco • Broadcasting in the United States: Innovative Challenge and Organizational
    Control
Vincent Mosco • Pushbutton Fantasies: Critical Perspectives on Videotext And Information
    Technology
Kaarle Nordenstreng and Herbert J. Schiller • National Sovereignty and International
    Communication: A Reader
Dan Schiller • Telematics and Government
Herbert I. Schiller • Who Knows: Information in the Age of the Fortune 500
Dallas W. Smythe • Dependency Road: Communications, Capitalism, Consciousness and
    Canada
Janet Wasko • Movies and Money: Financing the American Film Industry

In Preparation:

William C. Adams • Television Coverage of the 1980 Presidential Campaign
Mary B. Cassata and Thomas Skill • Life on Daytime Television
Badley S. Greenberg • Mexican Americans and the Mass Media
Kaarle Nordenstreng • The Mass Media Declaration of UNESCO
Jorge A. Schnitman • Dependency and Development in the Latin American Film Industries
Indu B. Singh • Telecommunications in the Year 2000: National and International
    Perspectives
Jennifer D. Slack • Communication Technologies and Society: Conceptions of Causality and
    the Politics of Technological Intervention
Osmo Wiio • Information and Communication Systems

Forecasting the Telephone:
A Retrospective Technology Assessment

by
Ithiel de Sola Pool

Research Program on Communications Policy
Massachusetts Institute of Technology

ABLEX Publishing Corporation
Norwood, New Jersey 07648

Library of Congress Cataloging in Publication Data

Pool, Ithiel de Sola, 1917–
    Forecasting the telephone.

    (Communication and information science)
    Includes bibliographical references and index.
    1. Technology assessment. 2. Technological forecasting. 3. Telephone.
I. Title. II. Series.
T174.5.P66   1982   303.4'833   82-22637
ISBN 0–89391–048-1

ABLEX Publishing Corporation
355 Chestnut Street
Norwood, New Jersey 07648

Contents

* Type A—The telephone will be used in manner x.

Type B—The telephone will be used in manner x, so society will be changed in manner y.

Type C—With wide use of phones, society will be changed in manner y.

Type D—Other propositions

Acknowledgements

This volume is based upon research papers written by Carolyn Cook, Craig Decker, Stephen Dizard, Kay Israel, David Ralston, Pamela Rubin, Barry Weinstein, and Thomas Yantek.

Without their work this book could not have been written, though the responsibility for the interpretation of their work must be fully borne by myself. The report was edited and typed by Suzanne Planchon.

This study was supported by a grant from the National Science Foundation.[1] It was one of a set of NSF-funded "retrospective technology assessments" of which the first to appear was on submarine telegraphy.[2]

Ithiel de Sola Pool

[1] Grant 7508807-A01-ERD

[2] Vary T. Coates and Bernard Finn. *A Retrospective Technology Assessment: Submarine Telegraphy—The Transatlantic Cable of 1866*. San Francisco: San Francisco Press, 1979.

Forecasting the Telephone:
A Retrospective Technology Assessment

I

Introduction

This is a book about forecasting. More specifically, it deals with forecasts about the telephone and what that new invention would do to society. These forecasts appeared between 1876, the year of Bell's invention, and 1940, by which time, in the United States, there was a mature telephone system in place. In those 65 years hundreds of forecasts were made. The magazines of the day were fond of discussing this exciting new technology and the revolution in life that it had produced. This attention was similar to that paid to the space program today. Both of these technologies caused revised conceptions of man's place in the universe.

The forecasts that appeared from 1876 to 1940 can be considered as a kind of "technology assessment." That phrase was not used in those days, but the objective was the same. Thinkers sought to assess the future of the phone and how it would change life. Sometimes they did well and sometimes they did badly. For us, in retrospect, the interesting question is to understand the successes and failures and the reasons for success or failure. What lessons can we learn from these early attempts at technology assessment?

THE THESIS

In successful technology assessment, market and technical analyses must be brought to bear simultaneously. Alone either of them fails; together they can produce some very prescient forecasts. That is the lesson gained from this case study of the telephone and its effects upon society.

1

The conclusion may sound banal, but if prevailing practice is any evidence, it is not. A large proportion of current technology assessments make little use of market analysis. Many of them compile expert evaluations of:

- available and likely technologies
- the potential uses of them
- their side effects
- their interaction with other alternative technologies and with social goals

without much serious effort toward a market analysis of the cost and demand for the alternatives. That sort of analysis, in the late 19th and early 20th centuries, resulted in some misled anticipations about the prospects of telephony. Some good assessments were also made, however, by people who focused simultaneously on the market and on technical features of the new technology.

Our study of the telephone is a case study, and like any case study, it does not provide extensional testing of its hypothesis. To define the boundaries within which our conclusion holds would require us to go beyond one case. Certainly, the telephone is not unique, but all we actually demonstrate here is that in the case of the telephone the crux of good technology assessment was and would have been the intimate melding of technical and market analyses.

We base that conclusion on a review and analysis of 186 forecasts about the social impact of the telephone system—some relatively prescient and some quite wrong. Before we look at those forecasts, however, let us consider the general concept of technology assessment and the place of forecasting in it.

THE CONCEPT OF TECHNOLOGY ASSESSMENT

Members of self-conscious disciplines are fond of debating the definition of their discipline. The younger and less recognized the discipline, the stronger that search for identity.

The debate about the definition of technology assessment is not one we choose to enter. It is not very useful to do more than note the kinds of things people do who call themselves practitioners of the art.

Technology assessors are interested in evaluating the social consequences of technological changes. They are forecasters. They seek to foresee not only which technological alternatives are likely to be adopted, but also what secondary consequences such adoption or non-adoption will have. The consequences of any technological development are partly other technical developments; for example, mastering the technology of electric circuits made possible the technology of telegraphy. Other consequences, however, are social; e.g., electricity was widely forecast to favor smaller plants than did steam power; based on that assumption, a dispersal of human aggregations was also predicted.[1]

Most technology assessments seek to catalog all the effects of a given technology, but some, on the other hand, seek to explore the technological conditions of a particular effect. Lord Ashby, for example, has studied the historical debate about smoke abatement legislation in Great Britain in the 19th century.[2]

Some authors make a distinction between technology forecasting and technology assessment, reserving the latter term for assessments of social consequences. We will make no such distinction here. Some technology assessments are highly normative, the assessment incorporating judgments of what is good or bad for society; such assessments are commonly made by environmental activists, for example. Other assessments are purely descriptive. Some assessments seek rigor by using various formal methodologies such as the Delphi technique or cross-impact analysis; others use the intuitive insights of historians or ethnologists.

What almost all who call themselves technology assessors share is a belief that if rational methods are used to anticipate consequences of different technical alternatives, better social choices can be made. That optimistic notion rests on two premises. One premise is that knowledge leads to more enlightened action; we shall not question this premise here. The second premise is that it is possible to forecast the consequences of technology with some success; this is the premise we seek to test in this case study.

It is not a foregone conclusion that forecasting of technology is feasible beyond a very limited time period and range of events. The argument for the infeasability of forecasting is that invention and discovery are by their nature surprise events. Indeed, it is sometimes said, if one can anticipate a discovery it is not a discovery.

We do not accept the logic of that argument. Almost every important invention and discovery has been anticipated in fantasy long before it was proven by practice or science. Mythology is full of men flying, walking on the moon, transmuting materials one to another, or communicating without being present. Each of these innovations was also discussed by serious scholars long before the particular ones who actually pulled off the trick of discovery or invention. Leonardo anticipated Orville Wright, though the conditions for successful realization did not exist. The word "Telephone" was used on a number of occasions throughout the 19th century by people who could conceive one, but not yet build one. We do not need to argue theoretically against the notion that discovery cannot be forecast. The issue is empirical. Some amazingly good forecasts have been made; that is a palpable fact that cannot be denied. We shall examine historically the circumstances in which, good or bad, the forecasts were made in a particular technical field, namely forecasts of the consequences of the telephone.

RETROSPECTIVE TECHNOLOGY ASSESSMENTS

This study is not itself a technology assessment as we have described that art above. It is a review of technology assessments that other people made over the past century. We ourselves make no effort to forecast or to evaluate possible consequences of future technologies. Our study is a historical one; it looks at the assessments that writers made in the past as they wrote about the telephone. We judge how good or bad the assessments were and try to distinguish what factors led to good assessments and what to bad. Finally we ask a "what if" question: if good methodologies had been followed and good data collected, how far could the consequences of the telphone (as we see them with our presumed 20/20 hindsight) have been anticipated in advance? That is why we call it a "retrospective technology assessment."[3] In a different social research tradition this might have been called a "gedanken-experiment," and in still other traditions it might have been called a study of "what if" or an examination of "counterfactuals."

The question before us is how, and how well, might observers at the turn of the century have anticipated the social impacts that the telephone has had?

Put that way, however, it is not a well defined question. It is, nonetheless, a type of question we ask all the time. Juries in damage cases try to decide if a defendant could reasonably have anticipated the consequences of what he did. A board of directors tries to decide whether a chief executive who has suffered a loss could properly have anticipated the market trends better than he did. When the medicine our physician prescribes fails to cure us, we ask ourselves whether he could have made a better diagnosis. In each such case we implicitly postulate a certain corpus of knowledge which the responsible actor should have used; we do not expect him to be omniscient. Until we define what knowledge base we expect him to have used, the question of what he could have known is an ill-defined one.

In the present study we ask what could have been anticipated about the impact of the telephone. We do not ask what a 1970s social scientist armed with the tools of econometric modelling, technology assessment, and survey research might have done if he were by some time warp wafted back to 1900. We propose a much more modest question: how well were people at that time able to anticipate consequences of the new technology, given only the knowledge and tools that existed in those days?

We chose this more modest question as our point of reference in part because answering it does not require us to engage in blue sky science fiction writing. By examining the analyses and forecasts that were actually made we can get some hold on the question of how well forecasters succeeded.

Within the constraints of the knowledge-base of their day, different observers made different forecasts—some good, some bad. The distribution of assessments that were actually made presumably represents the range from very nearly the best that anyone could reasonably have done at the time to somewhere near the worst. The question that we can fruitfully explore is: what led to good assessments and what to bad ones? What were the characteristics of the people who were good forecasters; what kinds of methods did they use; what kinds of data did they start from?

The answers to those questions have some practical value for the practice of technology assessment today. Granted, the existence of new analytic techniques and better data bases means that one would not today slavishly imitate even the best analyses of 1876-1940. Still, we have not made so much progress in social analysis that the lessons of that earlier period are irrelevant. If we can identify the ingredients that led to good technology assessments in that period, presumably the same general factors, *mutatis mutandis*, would be significant today.

A common naive assumption is that with the benefit of hindsight there should be no problem in grading a past forecast as right or wrong. In a previous publication this author has analyzed why that is not so.[4] On the one hand, very few assessments are stated unambiguously enough to be rigorously testable against the facts, and on the other hand, the facts themselves are often almost as hard to establish in retrospect as they are to forecast. Professional historians, after all, spend most of their time discovering and debating what past facts were.

The problem of testing the reliability of both predictions and postdictions can be illustrated by an example of typical difficulties. The telephone, it is often said today (and was said as early as the 1870s) is an invader of our privacy. (See Section 10.6 for a discussion of this topic.) There is no question that its imperious ring frequently interrupts domestic quiet. But the overall relation of the telephone to privacy is very complicated indeed, and it is hard to say whether its net effect has been to increase or decrease the extent of privacy in modern life. Early concerns about privacy had to do with listening in by operators on the line, accidentally crossed circuits, and, and above all, party lines. Comments on the telephone as a threat to privacy, when predicated on those features of the early phone system, might have been good analyses for those days, but poor forecasts for the era of the automatic dial phone. Yet concern about privacy persists, now focused partly on the matter of wiretapping. Indeed, intrusions on privacy by wiretapping are possible (perhaps more easily than steaming open of letters) and have occurred. But let us note some reverse aspects—those in which the telephone has improved privacy.

For one thing, the telephone permits confidential messages to be sent without the risks attendant on their commitment to writing. Besides that, the telephone has profoundly changed the mores regarding "dropping in." In the days before the telephone, intrusions on domestic seclusion took the form of someone dropping by. The polite thing in many circumstances was to call in person to pay one's respects. Conventions restricted this by time of day; also, servants might protect affluent masters with polite lies. But it is hard to argue that the ring of the phone—now in many circumstances a *de rigeur* precedent to visiting—is more intrusive on privacy than the physical arrival of a caller one hesitates to offend. Yet precisely because the phone call is so much lesser an intrusion than the unannounced visit that it replaced, it is indulged in much more frequently and undertaken more lightly.

So, given these various considerations (the great frequency of phone calls, their tendency to reduce unannounced visits, the privacy of the unwritten exchange, the small but existent possibility of tapping), what is the net impact of the telephone on privacy? And if one is to evaluate a turn of the century statement about the telephone and privacy, should one assume it to have been meant as a forecast stretching beyond the end of the operator and party line? Looking backward, are we any more sure what the effects of the phone have been on privacy than a forecaster would have been? Neither of us is sure.

Comparisons across time of judgments of the impact of the telephone, even if not easy, are nonetheless useful in giving us perspective. So are comparisons across space. We commissioned Professor Bertil Thorngren of the Stockholm School of Economics and Professor Michael Gibbons of the University of Manchester in England to search early sources of comment on the telephone in those countries. This cross-national comparison is important, because it is very easy in a study of one country (in this instance the United States) to misperceive some development as a natural consequence of the telephone itself, when it is in fact just one among alternative ways in which the device can be used. For example, is the phone a democratizing instrument or one which introduces a new element of status hierarchy? The U.S. experience, where the phone became fairly universal in half a century (and was always intended to be universal) provides considerable support (which we shall review below) for the view that the telephone has been a democratizing influence. In France and England phone penetration has gone much more slowly, and for a much longer period the telephone remained a prerogative of the rich. In 1904, there were 6.5 phones per hundred persons in Manhattan and Bronx, and 1.4 per hundred in London.[5] In 1912, when phone penetration in New York was 8.3 per 100 persons, and in Boston 9.2 per hundred, phone penetration in London was 2.8 per hundred. In 1914, when there were ten million phones in the U.S. There were 650,000 In Great Britain. Seventy percent of the world's phones were then in the U.S.

The extreme counter-example, however, is the Soviet Union, which has a very different phone system. Phone books are not made generally available, so unless one knows a person's number one can call only by using directory assistance, and many important numbers are not given out. The system, therefore, becomes to a great degree one of group communication within closed circles. That philosophy is further expressed in the existence of several segregated telephone networks for different institutions. The most significant is the "key" system which links members of the top elite, and which can only be dialed by someone with a key to unlock the instrument. In the Soviet Union the total of phones on the several segregated networks is apparently greater than that of the public network.

Just as a study of a single country could confuse one impact of the telephone with its necessary impact, so it may confuse the impact of other social circumstances with the impact of the telephone. For example, every modern country needs a good means of rapid dissemination of business information. If one looks only at the United States it is easy to believe that the telephone is the natural medium for that purpose. Perhaps it is. But other countries with less satisfactory phone systems tend to use alternative technologies to a greater extent than we do. There is a replacement effect. The European phone systems are less good and more expensive than the U.S. system; the European telex system is better and cheaper than that in the U.S. Correspondingly, European businessmen use telex much more frequently than Americans do, and use the phone less frequently.

Thus a second methodology that enters into our research to a certain degree is that of comparative analysis. One might design a study of the social impact of a technology like the telephone by systematic analysis of comparative data. Degrees of telephone penetration in different countries at different times could be correlated with various other social data. There are a number of studies of that kind on the subject of communication and development.[6] Various measures of penetration of telephones, newspapers, radios, and other communications media are found to correlate highly with indices of development. Causal models have been fitted to that multi-regression data.

There is, however, a problem to such a research design. Its validity depends upon a strong predominance of direct causal relations within each nation or other unit that is observed, over any interactions among those units. Let us explain the point by comparing the problems involved in testing two propositions about the telephone which are discussed later in this book: (1) The telephone fosters movement to suburbs, and (2) The manually switched telephone fostered women's liberation. Proposition 1 might very plausibly be sustained by a statistical comparison of the rate of telephone penetration and the rate of suburbanization between countries. For example the causal pattern might be thus:

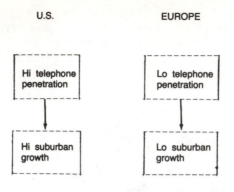

On the other hand, the causal pattern for telephone and women's liberation is likely to be more complex. What follows is an expository example, not a serious assertion about the fullness of reality.

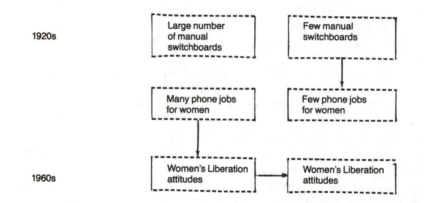

If that sort of pattern prevails to some significant degree, then a correlation, country by country, of manual switchboards with women's liberation would fail to appear, but to interpret that as denying that there had been a causal relationship would be an error. In the illustrative facts postulated in the diagram, manual switching did causally promote women's liberation in the United States, and via that, in Europe. So a causal relation is not refuted by the absence of a correlation across countries between manual switching and women's liberation.

For the most part the relationships of the telephone to society entail substantial interactions of the latter kind, which do not make a simple correlational analysis across countries very fruitful.

So the international comparisons that we have introduced into our research, while important, serve more to alert us to possible alternative paths of social development than to allow systematic correlational hypothesis testing.

The Procedure That We Followed

The data assembled for this study were assertions and forecasts that we found in writings between 1876 and 1940. Our data collection involved inventorying what social effects of the telephone were asserted; noting by whom, when, and where those effects were observed, or in some instances noting a failure to observe them; and attempting to identify the considerations or line of reasoning that went into those observations. Once that collection of statements was assembled, we attempted to evaluate the insightfulness of those informal technology assessments made during the course of the development of the telephone, and also to suggest how such anticipations could have been improved. There is clearly no simple mechanical way in which we can grade a series of forecasts for accuracy. As we have already noted, the statements in the record are too subject to interpretation, and the facts still too debatable. What we can do, and what we intend to do, is to list as many statements as seem to us to be reasonably arguable theses about the social impact of the telephone, then search the literature to find early and clear intimations of those impacts.

This is not an antiquarian search for the first man ever to make a certain statement. That futile enterprise is popular among scholars. Indeed it has been a popular game regarding the invention of the telephone. General Carty, the one-time Chief Engineer of AT&T, notes some claim that there was a 10th century inventor of the phone![7] We do search for early statements, because we are interested in how soon a particular social impact was perceived or anticipated. We are, however, equally or more interested in the clarity and fullness of the statements.

We are not interested in frequency counts of statements. It is relevant whether a certain observation was a rare perception or a common comment. But there is no well defined universe for which we could create a sensible sample frame, allowing a rigorous count; nor would that have been valuable if it were possible. Any statement anyone made in the early years of the telephone is grist for our mill if it said anything significant by way of assessment of that technology. For us to find it today, the statement would have to have been preserved—perhaps in a book or an article, perhaps in a newspaper story, perhaps in the transcripts of legislative or administrative proceedings, perhaps in a private letter, perhaps on a phonograph disc[8] or moving picture. For us the appropriate search rule was to search where the ore was likely to be richest, not to sample the universe; that would have been appropriate if our question concerned a frequency distribution. The use of overall sampling where the purpose is to find a particular nugget is well described in the familiar fallacy of the drunkard's search—the drunk who looks for his lost key under the streetlight because the light is better, not where he thinks he dropped it.

The places we did search, because we thought the ore was rich, were many: *The New York Times Index;* popular magazines covered in *Reader's Guide* and other periodical indexes; books on the telephone as an institution; on AT&T, on the invention of the telephone and on the lives of Bell, Vail and other key figures; sociological books from before World War II on communication and social change; FCC reports on relevant topics, most particularly the Walker Report;[9] trade journals, of which *Telephony* proved most valuable; leading treatises on the fields of the dependent variables in our propositions (e.g., urban planning, police work, fire prevention, economic history, political campaigning, and diplomacy) to see what they said about the telephone.

A fortuitous event that aided this project was the coincidence of the centenary of the telephone with our research. A centenary convocation was held at MIT under the sponsorship of AT&T. The author was in charge of a symposium there on the social impact of the telephone. This permitted him to invite about 20 papers from leading scholars on various aspects of the telephone in society during the past century.[10] Many important sources and insights emerged from that exercise.

It should be emphasized that our purpose in this study is something other than *testing* hypotheses about the telephone. We are about to *state* a large number of such hypotheses, ask who put them forward, when, and under what circumstances there was good analysis of them. There is no implication that all of these hypotheses are necessarily valid, although to some degree most of them probably are. We are ennumerating hypotheses, not affirming them. In some instances we shall even list contradictory hypotheses. All that we affirm is that these hypotheses are important enough, and have support enough so that a historical review of a technology assessment should explore them.

The list of hypotheses that we are about to present is by no means exhaustive. What criteria did we apply in making this inventory? First of all we were concerned with *social* effects of the telephone—not with its purely technical effects, nor with the social effects of the policies and behavior of AT&T. Either of those lists would be a much longer one. Bell Labs has produced two thick volumes of a series on the history of Bell System technical accomplishments.[11] There are literally tens of thousands of technical developments that can trace some part of their ancestry back to research and development for the telephone system. So too, the list of social effects that AT&T as an organization has had in every city and town in the United States could go on indefinitely. AT&T happens to be an enlightened company which for several decades has encouraged participation of its executives in cultural programs for overall enrichment. We do not consider that choice of policies by AT&T to be an effect of the telephone. The adoption of such policies was an option that any top management could have made, or alternatively could have rejected. For inclusion of any social phenomenon in our inventory we have to see some causal chain tracing the effect back to the technology itself.

Furthermore, our inventory is of effects that were discussed, assessed, or denied in the period from 1876 to 1940. That means we would generally miss any effects which occurred but which were not noticed. We have included only a couple of points that have been largely overlooked, because they seemed to us so very important that their oversight itself was significant. But those are exceptions.

Thus the primary criteria for inclusion of an hypothesis in our inventory were that (a) it is an assertion about the social impact of telephone technology, (b) it is at least moderately important, and (c) some discussion of it occurred in the early telephone years.

One last point: when we talk of the impact of "the telephone" we use that phrase as shorthand for the telephone system. We are not studying just the effects of the handset, but rather the effects of a switched point-to-point network of voice communication in the society.

A Review Of The Inventory

In this introduction, it seems fit to summarize a few of the more striking social effects of the telephone that we shall discuss more fully in the central part of the book.

Among the most significant impacts of the telephone were those in modifying the pattern of human settlement. It made farm life less isolated, made suburbs more practical, helped break up single industry neighborhoods, allowed offices of industrial companies to move away from the plant into downtown office buildings, and made skyscrapers economic. A parallel set of effects operated on businesses and bureaucratic organizations. Creation of large units and decentralized management of them were both facilitated by telecommunications. The labor requirements of the growing telephone system stimulated technical education and also employment of women. Telephone canvassing changed marketing and politics. Telephone reporting changed the relation of journalists and editors. Field telephones extended the range of command and control in warfare. The growth of telephony caused both the telegraph and postal services to run into the red. Out of telephone research grew many new technologies such as the transistor and computers. Using the telephone system many new business services sprang up, such as answering services and taxi calling. The telephone changed social habits and etiquette in such matters as calling upon strangers. These are simply a few among 186 impacts we discuss later.[12]

We have stated above our major conclusion, namely that for a large class of technologies *a technical—economic market analysis is the place to begin in successful technology assessment.* A taxonomy of 186 propositions found in the inventory that is to follow establishes a particular structure of precedence and dependence among the asserted patterns of causation.

About half of all the propositions (91 out of the 186) take the form of forecasting that the new telephone technology would be used in a certain way; the reasoning behind these forecasts almost always involved a market analysis. For example, it was seen that the phone could be used by company officers to locate their offices downtown while at the same time keeping in touch with their plant on the outskirts. It was also forecast that the phone would be used to listen to concerts without leaving home. Of these two forecasts, one was right and one wrong. The logic of both arguments, however, was that there were enough people ready to pay what the service would have to cost, given the technology available, so that the service could be successfully offered.[13]

Fifty-two more of the propositions use the same logic but carry it one step forward. The logic underlying the 91 above-mentioned propositions had the form:

> Given alternative technologies, their costs, and consumer demand, the technology will be used in manner X.

The 52 additional propositions had the form:

> The technology will be used in manner X, and so society will be changed in manner Y.

To illustrate: A proposition of the first type was that the telephone would be used to keep in touch with physicians on their rounds. A proposition of the second type was that because the phone could keep their offices in touch with physicians on their rounds, medical neighborhoods would break up since co-location of doctors was no longer necessary.

Thus 143 of the 186 propositions are directly derived from a technical and economic analysis of the market.[14] Of the remaining 43 propositions, which do not rest on telephone market analysis, 36 have the logical form:

> Given that telephones come to be widely used, society will be changed in manner Y.

These last propositions do not rest upon a market analysis of demand for a particular use of the phone, but only on the prevalence of the phone in general. Examples of these 36 propositions are the assertions that letter writing and handwriting would deteriorate in the telephone age.

Five of the residual seven propositions are psychological. These are the assertions that women would talk more on the phone than men, that young people would talk more than old, that young people would use the phone for safe sexuality, that people would prefer a private earphone to a loudspeaker phone, and that the ability to talk to a distance would erode an orthodox religious view of the universe. Finally, there are the propositions that the telephone was used by authors (particularly of drama) as a device for bringing remote agents into their plots, and that understanding of telephony would lead to understanding of telepathy.

Any classification of complex ideas is interpretive and subject to error. Readers will argue that we have misclassified some propositions; probably so. One would have to disagree on a large number of cases, however, to change the main conclusions. For those who are bothered by some of the decisions we made, they are all on record in the text, the reader can revise them if he wishes and draw conclusions accordingly.

In Part II, we present the inventory of propositions about the impact of the telephone. Here, as in the listing of the contents, each item in the inventory is classified as follows:

Type A	Telephone will be used in manner x.	Type C	With wide use of phones, society will be changed in manner y.
Type B	Telephone will be used in manner x, so society will be changed in manner y.	Type D	Other propositions.

The outline that we have followed in the inventory organizes the substantive contents of the forecasts in one particular way. Any such outline is partly unsatisfactory, for cross-cutting topics may be relevant in more than one place. Rather than following the literary convention of avoiding repetitions, we have chosen to adhere strictly to the chosen outline of forecasts. The reader may be bothered by a few repetitious topics, wherever the same developments contributed to more than one effect. Effects of the telephone on government and on business, for example, appear at different points in the outline. But both the state and the firm are large organizations, so the effect of the telephone in facilitating large scale institutions is noted in two places.

Generally we state propositions in the future tense, as if they were forecasts at the time that they were stated. But when a proposition may have been a significant trend primarily at the early time when it was observed, and especially if it is no longer so, we drop into present or even past tense. Our symbolic use of tenses should not be confused with any implication that the authors, whose writings we are analyzing, formulated their expressions in this way. They were writing for their purposes, not ours. We are often imposing a reconstruction on what they wrote to turn their statements into forecasts. Many explicit forecasts exist. General John J. Carty, a key figure in American telephone development, wrote an anonymous column called "The Prophet's Corner" in the journal *Electrical Engineering,* and H.G. Wells wrote a book of forecasts for the 20th century called *Anticipations.* [15] More often, however, the statements that we have framed as forecasts were analyses of newly emergent trends which the author clearly expected to keep going.

One conclusion, already labelled as our central thesis, seems inescapable from this retrospective look at the forecasts that were made:

> A successful and comprehensive technology assessment of the tele-
> phone would have had to start with an informed analysis of the technologi-
> cal prospects and possibilities of the device, coupled with a good market
> analysis of demand for different types of phone and phone service. If from
> that one anticipated that there would be extensive use of the telephone for
> certain functions or extensive use of it in general, then one could draw
> further inferences about how that would affect society.

The conclusion that we have drawn about the requirements for a good telephone assessment holds particularly because the telephone was introduced as a consumer product.

For some technologies which are not consumer products a different mode of analysis would be relevant. It is important to note that S. Myers and D.G. Marquis found that 75 percent of 567 innovations were a response to market needs or manufacturing economy. [16] Still, the residual quarter of the cases were not such a response.

Some assessments among these non-consumer products would be quite similar to those of the consumer products except that the sponsors, whose economic support had to be assured, were not the general public. A technology assessment of a weapons system, for example, also requires a market analysis, but the consumers whose favor must be won are governments.

Ideologists have tried to lay down philosophically based rules about what historians, sociologists, or technology assessors ought to study. We are not trying to establish such rules. We have tried to be empirical, cataloguing what people have found worthwhile to say about the impact of the telephone. When we do that, we discover—not surprisingly—that the majority of interesting propositions ask both what was technically possible and also who was ready to pay how much for that.

In the case of telecommunications, as in many other technologies, a variety of alternative means were available to meet the basic human need being served, in this instance rapid remote communication. The choice among technological alternatives as to which to use, and in which ways they should be used, was determined in almost every case by an economic-technical set of considerations. There were technical parameters as to what was possible, but almost always several alternatives were within the range of possibility. What actually emerged was determined by what could be effectively marketed, what activities capital could be raised for, and what arrangements would allow for efficient billing—in short, by economic considerations.

Often when new technologies are introduced, choices are made in the light of currently visible costs and benefits which foreclose alternatives that later on appear desirable. For example, use of narrow bandwidth in the phone system to make phoning cheap for conversations later precluded video delivery by phone. One cannot do everything, and every choice made to optimize for one purpose has drawbacks for other purposes.

One evaluation a retrospective technology assessment can make is to identify which of those early decisions later turn out to be mistakes. Not every such penalty on the future for the sake of the present is a mistake, however.

Today, when cable television is being adopted to meet the public's demand for a wider choice of video material, we wish that the universal telephone network had been designed to accommodate those broader band signals, but no rational decision maker would have burdened past generations with the cost of a more expensive system than they needed for the sake of satisfying a want that is just now emerging. So too, receivers of nuisance phone calls today may wish that the phone system had been designed to make it possible to identify the source of a call from the receiving end. Now that "junk" advertising calls are becoming common, that would be particularly useful as a means of allowing the recipient to filter calls. With the coming of integrated digital telephone networks with common control signalling, that facility can be cheaply provided. But in an analog system with in-band signalling, the cost of acquiring that additional information would have been considerable. In the first century of the telephone, the only information that needed to be kept on who was calling was billing information for toll calls. To have burdened the system with the extra cost of retaining knowledge at the receiving end of who was calling whom, would have levied a high charge on early users for needs as yet dimly perceived, for the benefit of generations as yet unborn.

Sometimes, however, we can in retrospect say that a mistake was made, i.e., that incurring the added costs for a different system would have proved to be the wise choice. Thus in the energy field one can point to building designs and numerous other investments that would have been made or made differently in the 1960s if one had anticipated the energy shortage of 1973 and the rise in the price of oil. We cannot point to such clear cases or obvious mistakes in the history of the telephone.

Whether the choices made were wise ones or mistakes, the pervasive process of choosing present economy at someone else's later cost was visible throughout the telephone's development. In the history of the telephone, the tradeoff between economy now and capacity for adaption to novel needs in the future was generally made in favor of meeting demands that were predictable in the time frame that an investor would consider.

Telephone service was introduced as a commodity. The decisions faced were marketing decisions. What ended up being provided was whatever entrepreneurs could see a prospect of selling at a profit. Costs for facilities for which there was little market demand were eliminated wherever possible. For example, we shall note later that facilities which would have been useful in crime control and fire fighting were not provided on the universal switched system because city police and fire departments were not promising customers. One cannot fault telephone entrepreneurs for that decision. On the whole they judged well and accurately what the market demanded. They created a universal phone system by meeting that demand at a modest price. To put it more accurately, the entrepreneurs who succeeded acted in that way. There were plenty of dreams over the past century about things that the telephone might do, but which it did not do. The developers whose forecasts and plans embodied those dreams fell by the wayside. The phone was a consumer commodity, and its course was charted by market demand that could be felt within a modest time frame.

The best forecasts, it is interesting to note, arose from people involved in the industry. That is where we find people who understood the technology, who also sought to assess how to implement it in a way that would pay.

FOOTNOTES

[1]Frederick A. C. Perrine, Electrical Engineering and Social Reform. *Electrical Engineering*, 1894, *3*, (2) 39.

[2]Eric Ashby and Mary Anderson. Studies in the Politics of Environmental Protection: The Historical Roots of the British Clean Air Act, 1956. *Interdisciplinary Science Review*, 1976, (4) 279-290 and 1977, 28 (1) 9-26.

[3]Vary T. Coates and Bernard Finn, *A Retrospective Technology Assessment: Submarine Telegraphy*, San Francisco: San Francisco Press, 1979; Joel A. Tarr (ed.). *Retrospective Technology Assessment.* San Francisco: San Francisco Press, 1976.

[4] Ithiel Pool. Alternatives in Social Science Forecasting. In Nazli Choucri and Thomas Robinson (Eds.), *Forecasting in International Relations: Theory, Methods, Problems, Prospects.* San Francisco: W.H. Freeman, 1978.

[5] Merchants' Association of New York, *Inquiry Into Telephone Service and Rates* 1905.

[6] Such studies are reviewed by Frederick Frey. Communication and Development. In I. Pool and W. Schramm (Eds.), *Handbook of Communication.* Chicago: Rand McNally, 1973.

[7] Carty in 1891 alluded to a common unsubstantiated assertion that the telephone, presumably the string or "Lovers" telephone, had been invented by the ancient Chinese at the time of Confucious. (John J. Carty. *Electrical Review,* August 22, 1891, 13 (26), 334.)

[8] One such is "Cohen on the Telephone," cited in Martin Mayer. The Telephone and the Uses of Time. In Ithiel Pool (Ed.), *The Social Impact of the Telephone*. Cambridge: MIT Press, 1976, p. 240.

[9] Federal Communications Commission, *Investigation of the Telephone Industry in the United States*. U.S. Government Printing Office, 1957. (Also published as 76th Congress, 1st Session, House Document No. 340; Reprinted by Arno Press, 1975.)

[10] Pool. *The Social Impact of the Telephone*.

[11] M.D. Fagen (Ed.). *A History of Engineering in the Bell System* (2 vols.). New York: Bell Telephone Laboratories, 1975)1978.

[12] The inventory consists of 186 propositions and 40 headings. They are listed in sequence in the Contents and organized by type.

[13] In four of the 91 cases, while economic as well as technical considerations were important, the economic considerations were internal cost considerations rather than consumer demand considerations. Thus, for example, the failure of the phonograph to be used as telephone repeater was because other technologies could do the job better more cheaply.

[14] We did two independent content analyses of the inventory. The first count found 127 out of 181 propositions fitting that model; on the second count the result was 143 out of the 185. There is, of course, a margin of judgment ix the classification. The discrepancy is twelve disagreements plus four cases that were placed in a category added in the second count that had to do with internal costs rather than market demand. In this report we use the figures from the second count because in it we subdivided some of the earlier categories for more refined analysis.

[15] H.G. Wells. *Anticipations*, New York: Harper Bros., 1902).

[16] S. Myers and D.G. Marquis, *Successful Industrial Innovations* (NSF 69-17). Washington D.C.: National Science Foundation, May 1969.

Inventory of Propositions on the Impact of the Telephone

1

Prognoses for Telephone Development

We start with forecasts about the development of the telephone system itself, for the shape of the system to come would determine its social impact.

Perhaps the most remarkable single forecast of the future of the telephone is in a letter that Alexander Graham Bell wrote to a group of British investors as early as 1878, just two years after his invention. It describes a universal point-to-point service connecting everyone through a central office in each community, which in turn would be connected by long distance lines.

At the present time we have a perfect network of gas pipes and water pipes throughout our large cities. We have main pipes laid under the streets communicating by side pipes with the various dwellings, enabling the members to draw their supplies of gas and water from a common source.

In a similar manner it is conceivable that cables of telephone wires would be laid under ground, or suspended overhead, communicating by branch wires with private dwellings, counting houses, shops, manufactories, etc., uniting them through the main cable with a central office where the wire could be connected as desired, establishing direct communication between any two places in the city. Such a plan as this, though impracticable at the present moment, will, I firmly believe, be the outcome of the introduction of the telephone to the public. Not only so, but I believe in the future wires will unite the head offices of telephone companies in different cities, and a man in one part of the country may communicate by word of mouth with another in a distant place.[1]

1.1 The telephone will become pervasive.

From the start Bell and his colleagues foresaw the telephone as a widely distributed consumer service. The Bell letter and various similar statements anticipated the prospect of millions of phones. Numerous articles from 1900 on projected the observed growth curve.[2]

1.1.1 The telephone will become "universal." (Type A)

The word "universal" was part of Vail's favorite slogan: "One policy, one system, and universal service", used by him, for example, in AT&T's 1909, 1910 and 1911 Annual Reports:

> The Bell system was founded on broad lines of "One System," "One Policy," "Universal Service," on the idea that no aggregation of isolated independent systems not under common control, however well built or equipped, could give the country the service that an interdependent, inter-communicating, universal system could give. One system with a common policy, common purpose and common action; comprehensive, universal, interdependent, intercommunicating like the highway system of the country, extending from every door to every other door, affording electrical communication of every kind, from every one at every place to every one at every other place. (1910)[3]

There is a certain ambiguity. "Universal" implied either to "everyone," or to "everywhere," without clear specification.

1.1.2 The telephone will be used by the poor. (Type A)

A clearer formulation of the expectation that the phone would reach virtually every home was contained in statements that the phone would become cheap enough to be used by the poor. Graham Bell, talking about automatic exchanges, said they will "so reduce the expense that the poorest man cannot afford to be without this telephone."[4]

The price of phone service when that prediction was made was very high. At such prices phone service could never have become universal. In 1882 the New York residential rate had been $150 a year, and in Chicago, Philadelphia, and Boston $100.[5] In New York City in 1896 phone service cost $20 a month, compared to the average worker's income of $38.50 a month.

It was recognized by both the Bell System and the independents that achieving the goal of wide or universal service depended on finding a way to reduce the cost of service for ordinary users. One solution was the pay phone, the first of which was introduced in Springfield, Mass. in 1883. Six years later, in 1889, the coin phone was introduced in Hartford, Conn. By 1902, 81,000 (3½%) of the 2,315,000 phones in service in the U.S. were pay phones.[6]

Another solution was metered service. The problem was to bring the price of service down for the small user while still collecting adequate amounts from businesses and large users. In 1896 the New York phone company introduced message unit charges.

One solution, adopted by many rural independent companies but rejected by the Bell System, was to create rudimentary small scale systems for local service only. These minimal systems, which were often built and maintained by farmers for themselves, commonly retained no reserve for depreciation, sometimes used fence wires for transmission, used party lines, and had a primitive exchange, often with only part time manning. Such systems could be very cheap if they stayed small and were not interconnected. (cf. Section 2.2.3.2)[7]

A basic assumption of Graham Bell's that was shared by the later developers of the independent rural systems was that the basic telephone device was a simple one, lending itself to a low cost service. In particular the contrast between telephony and telegraphy was often noted. While the Morse key instrument too was simple, the transmission of code required a professional operator, and therefore the lines went only to telegraph offices, not to homes and places of work. In section 7.2.1 we shall take note of the attempts of telegraphers to break out of that constraint by using electrical call bells to summon telegraph boys and by the installation of cumbersome printing telegraphs.[8] Here we need only note that the requirement for a device that could be wired to every home and office for direct instantaneous use was recognized early.

In 1846, *Punch* (vol. 11, p. 253) argued that telegraphy was "too good a thing to be confined to public use" and that it should be introduced into "the domestic circle." In 1848 (vol 15, p. 275) it reported (wrongly) that in the U.S. songs were being sent by telegraph from Boston to New York: "It must be delightful for a party at Boston to be able to call upon a gentleman in New York for a song." In 1858 (vol. 35 p. 254) it returned to the theme of a telegraph with lines reaching to the customer, or at least "within a hundred yards of every man's door." "With a house telegraph," *Punch* concluded, "it would be a perpetual tete-a-tete."[9]

Telephone enthusiasts like Bell may have anticipated a service that would be cheap enough to serve everyone, including the poor, but that expectation was not shared by all. Phone service as it actually existed in the early days was a luxury for the rich, and many people expected it to stay just that. Various quotations can be found minimizing the value and economic prospects of the telephone.[10]

> I fancy the descriptions we get of its use in America are a little exaggerated, though there are conditions in America which necessitate the use of such instruments more than here. Here we have a superabundance of messengers, errand boys and things of that kind. . . . The absence of servants has compelled America to adopt communications systems for domestic purposes. Few have worked at the telephone much more than I have. I have one in my office, but more for show. If I want to send a message—I use a sounder or employ a boy to take it.[11]

> The assistant Postmaster General could scarcely believe that a man of Vail's sound judgment, one who holds an honorable and far more responsible position than any man under the Postmaster General, should throw it up for a d--d old Yankee notion (a piece of wire with two Texas steer horns attached to the ends with an arrangement to make the concern bleat like a calf) called a telephone.[12]

Such expectations, when held by those in power, tended to be self-fulfilling prophecies. The development of a widespread low-cost phone system depended upon sympathetic treatment by the law. In the U.S. the telegraph law that was applied (see Section 4.3.1) was largely supportive of the phone companies, encouraging entrepreneurs to go into business and providing them with rights of way for stringing up lines. In other countries such as England and France the governments' assumptions about the phone systems' potential utility were quite different, and legal policies were restrictive.

In France a basic assumption was that the primary function of telecommunications was national defense. Service to private citizens was subordinated. The phone (especially a diffused network) was considered to have certain disadvantages from a security point of view as compared with the telegraph.[13] In Britain the phone was seen as a businessman's convenience which threatened the national investment in the telegraph system. Even after nationalization of the phone system (in 1912) Labor critics sometimes objected to the Post Office using its funds to build up the businessman's telephone instead of the common man's means of communication, the post.[14]

A crucial factor underlying predictions about telephone diffusion was the forecaster's expectation about potential trends in the cost of service. The expectations themselves, however, had to some degree the character of self-fulfilling prophecies. In the U.S., where a system of low cost universal service was anticipated from an early date, such a system was in fact created. Where there were less sanguine expectations about the telephone's general utility and economy, the system grew more slowly and has not become universal even today.

1.2 Telephony will be a switched service offered as a public utility. (Type A)

The device Bell invented could have been marketed in various ways. One of the first issues that Bell and his backers, Hubbard and Sanders, had to resolve was whether to sell or rent phones.[15] The decisive development that shaped the decision and the system was the switchboard, introduced to telephony in 1878.[16] It made a range of interconnections possible that would not otherwise have been feasible. In 1894 Arthur Vaughan Abbott calculated that a system of 10,000 subscribers (the approximate number then in New

York or Chicago) would have required underground ducts a yard square, or a pole 1000 feet high, if a separate line had to go between each pair of subscribers.[17] Before the switchboard, pairs of phones, connected a business office and factory or businessman's home and office, but the potential utility of such intercoms, which could well have been sold, was far less than that of a switched phone system, which almost had to run as a billed utility service.[18]

The first phone switchboard was in New Haven, and came about almost accidentally. The local Bell licensee ran all the wires from his subscribers' pairs of phones through his office for ease of servicing. The inadvertent crossing of connections between subscribers quickly suggested a new and useful service.[19]

When the switchboard idea came to Bell's attention in a letter from John Ponton he reacted with pleasure, commenting that that was the way he had always anticipated the system developing.[20] Indeed, his 1877 lectures predicted that people would phone each other to chat in a way that implied a switched system[21] His 1878 letter talking of the phone as a utility presents the same picture.

Thus, very early, the Bell System pioneers developed the conception of what Vail in 1879 called the "grand telephonic system."

This is the system for which Vail's slogan was "one system, one policy, and universal service." The key elements of the concept of the "grand system" was that phone service should be provided by a monopoly, either of one national company "owning and operating the whole system," or of a series of affiliated regional companies "under the control of one central organization"[22] (which ended up being the company with the long lines); that all exchanges should be interconnected; that rates should be set at a level to provide amortization of capital and an attractive return; that high quality reliable service should be provided; and that universal coverage of the country should be achieved with service offered on a public utility basis to all persons.

The most controverted of those propositions was the advocacy of a monopoly, an issue we discuss in section 4.4. The independents argued for the merits of competition and anticipated that there would be rival phone companies in operation. The "grand system" could have included telegraphy too, for the same wires could carry both phone calls and telegraphic messages. (cf. Section 7.2.3.) Indeed Bell and Vail conceived it that way.[23] It did not develop that way, but it did develop into a large, and in its area of operation, mostly monopolistic public utility.

1.2.1 Switching will be automatic. (Type A)

Until as late as the 1920s there was some debate as to the relative merits of an automatic as opposed to a manual switching system. Social impacts and utilities are very different for a system in which a human operator is an intermediary and one without an operator. Later in this book we shall discuss operators in relation to the role of women (9.4.2), privacy (10.6), emergency services (5.2), information and advisory services on the telephone (8.2.2 and 2.2.1.6), and loneliness and sense of community (9.1.1). In all those respects operators performed a helpful function.

But operators also had many disadvantages. It was a fit of pique at an operator whom he believed to be discriminating against him, that led Strowger to invent the automatic switch in 1889. The first automatic exchange was established in La-Porte, Indiana, in 1892.

In some countries of Europe automatic switching was introduced more rapidly than in the United States. In Europe it spread after 1900;[24] in the U.S. among the independents a decade later, and in the Bell System two decades later. The Bell System in the U.S. had the largest sunk investment in manually switched plant. It had just converted to French central power phones and was reluctant to use scarce capital to make a second shift. Also in some European countries (e.g., France) women proved less willing to take operator jobs than in America. Also, language diversities in some places in Europe made dialing attractive.

The decisive reason for the ultimate introduction of automatic switching was the growth in the size of the phone network to the point where it would have required an infeasible number of operators. A general characteristic of networks is that the links increase combinatorially with the number of nodes. That basic fact was noted early by phone companies which found that the cost of service increased as systems grew. Tiny rural exchanges could charge much less than the $20 a month charged in 1896 in New York City. Dilts quotes an early telephone manager: "All he had to do was get enough subscribers and the company would go broke."[25]

Financial Notes of 1905 quotes Graham Bell as arguing that as the number of people in an exchange increases, the operators' work goes up exponentially; hence sooner or later exchanges will have to be automated. So as the network grew it became obvious that the transition to automatic switching would have to be made some day.

While the transition to automatic switching was seriously delayed in the United States by financial problems of AT&T, competition was a stimulus to action. In 1912, the Automatic Electric Company, an independent phone company, claimed 300,000 phones on automatic exchanges.[26] The Home Telephone company, another major competitor, had a dial patent; in 1910 AT&T absorbed it. After 1920 the Bell System finally began to shift to dial phones. By 1936 48% of U.S. phones were on automatic exchanges. In Europe by 1939 the figure was 64%.

1.3   Long distance service will be provided. (Type A)

The original telephones of the 1870s could operate over a range of about 20 miles. Yet from the start almost everyone who talked about telephony seemed to assume that it was only a matter of time before very long distance or even global communication could be achieved. As quoted at the beginning of this chapter, Bell in his 1878 letter declared that through wired connections between telephone offices in different cities, long distance telephone communication would become possible.[27]

Even earlier, long range communication was assumed by Sir William Thomson (later Lord Kelvin), when judging the technical exhibits at the Philadelphia Exposition in 1876. Though most of his report covers which words he had been able to understand and which he could not, using the primitive device at hand, he assumed that eventually the device would improve enough to function at a distance.[28]

Similar expectations appeared in lay journals. The *Springfield Republican* observed on February 15, 1877;

> The music of a prima donna could be distributed over the country . . .
> or the fluteplaying of an amateur, may be heard around the world.[29]

The telephone entrepreneurs had a different vision of the telephone's usage, but not of its ability to transcend distance. Vail also anticipated a far flung global telephone network, and saw that strategic control would lie with the company running the long-line interconnections. "Tell our agents," he wrote to one of his staff in 1879, "that we have a proposition on foot to connect the different cities for the purpose of personal communication, and in other ways to organize a grand telephonic system."[30] Vail also said:

> We may confidentially expect that Mr. Bell will give us the means of
> making voice and spoken words audible through the electric wire to an ear
> hundreds of miles distant.[31]

A commentator noted that:

> This prophecy was expressed in the certificate of incorporation of the
> American Telephone and Telegraph Company formed in 1885 which certi-
> fied that the general route of lines of this association . . . will connect one
> or more points in each and every city, town or place in the State of New
> York with one or more points in each and every other city, town or place in
> said state, and in each and every other of the United States, and in Canada
> and Mexico; and each and every other of said cities, towns and places is to
> be connected with each and every other city, town or place in said states
> and countries, and also by cable and other appropriate means with the rest
> of the known world.[32]

The first long distance line was built between Boston and Lowell in 1880 with Vail's encouragement.

> This success cheered Vail on to a master effort. He resolved to build a
> line from Boston to Providence, and was so stubbornly bent upon doing

this that, when the Bell Company refused to act, he organized a company and built the line. (1881) It was a failure at first and went by the name of "Vail's Folly." But one of the experts, by a happy thought, doubled the wire, . . .

At once the Bell Company came over to Vail's point of view, bought his new line, and launched out upon what seemed to be the foolhardy enterprise of stringing a double wire from Boston to New York. This was to be a line de luxe, built of glistening red copper, not iron. Its cost was to be $70,000, which was an enormous sum in those hard-scrabble days. There was much opposition to such extravagance and much ridicule.

But when the last coil of wire was stretched into place, and the first "Hello" leaped from Boston to New York, the new line was a success.[33]

By 1892 there were lines from New York to Chicago, by 1911 from New York to Denver, and by 1915 from New York to San Francisco. Experiments with overseas radio telephony took place in 1915, but the first trans-Atlantic commercial service began only in 1927.[34] While long distance telephony grew rapidly, Bell's and Vail's predictions preceded its reality. There were many technical difficulties, and not everyone anticipated (as did Bell and Vail) that they would be overcome.

Much of the effort to make long distance telephony work focused on repeaters, devices which rebuilt the deteriorating and fading signals that passed through long lengths of wire. Berliner developed one. Hammond Hayes, the Director of the Mechanical Department, decided that the company could most economically abandon its own fundamental research and instead rely on "the collaboration with the students of the Institute of Technology and probably of Harvard College."[35] On research concerned with long lines, however, Hayes made an exception (cf. Section 8.1). He employed George A. Campbell, who had been educated at MIT and Harvard, to study the essentially mathematical problem of maintaining transmission constants over long lines of cable. By 1899, Campbell had outlined the nature of discretely loaded electrical lines and had developed the basic theory of the wave filter.

Around 1900, Pupin at Columbia University developed the loading coil, which greatly improved the capabilities of long distance cable. Before 1900, long distance lines demanded wire about 1/8 inch thick; the New York—Chicago line consumed 870,000 pounds of copper wire. Underground wires in particular had to be very thick. One fourth of all the capital invested in the telephone system before 1900 had been spent on copper. With the Pupin coil, the diameter of the wire could be cut in half (cf. Section 6.3). Then, in 1907, the vacuum tube used in repeaters made long distance communication increasingly economical.

Vail wrote in the 1908 annual report:

It took courage to build the first toll line—short as it was—and it took more to build the first long-distance line to Chicago. If in the early days the immediate and individual profit of the long-distance toll lines had been considered, it is doubtful if any would have been built."[36]

One obvious speculation as to why the forecast of long distance communication was so successfully made by Bell and Vail is that the telegraph shaped their thinking; the telephone's invention, after all, had been a by-product of telegraphy. Bell had been employed to create a harmonic telegraph which would carry messages at different pitches simultaneously. The telegraph's great achievement had been the contraction of distance; it was not surprising, therefore, that when a way was found to make voice travel over wires, its transmission over distance seemed a realizable goal. Quite rightly, telephone enthusiasts saw the technical problems as temporary difficulties.[37] The sanguine expectations based on the telegraph analogy also led to some bad predictions that slid too easily over technical and economic realities.[38] In an interview with the *New York Sun*, printed February 20, 1877, Thomas Watson, Bell's assistant, stated that he had not the slightest doubt that in a few months a man could lecture in Boston and be heard by an audience in any part of the country.

> No trial has been made, however, of the transmission of sounds to so great a distance as across the Atlantic. Mr. Watson said that as far as they had been able to ascertain, there seemed to be a limit to the distance over which the sounds could be made to travel; but he expressed himself as confident that in due time any given distance could be annihilated.[39]

In May, 1877 the Springfield Republican said:

> We have grown so used to new and marvelous additions to the power of telegraphy that nothing seems impossible, and Professor Bell's confident expectation that he will shortly be able to send his voice across the Atlantic and talk with men 3,000 miles away as readily as if they were in the next room, meets with no . . . satiric hearing . . .[40]

The word "shortly" in the quotation is more likely the journalist's license than Bell's own. Yet even General Carty, later chief engineer of the Bell System, who should have had his eye firmly fixed on the problems of attenuation and repeaters, forecast a New York–San Francisco link by 1900,[41] fifteen years ahead of the reality.

1.4   Forecasts about technological alternatives.

The components of a point-to-point communication system are terminals at the ends, a transmission medium linking them, and a switching center in the middle. There are many different things that can be done by a system of that conception, and many different types of hardware that can be used. The hardware chosen affects the practicable uses. A loudspeaker, for example, would be more relevant to a system used for broadcast than to one for point-to-point messages.

1.4.1   A switched teletypewriter system will be provided. (Type A)

Printing telegraphs existed before the telephone. In the 1840s in the U.S. the House printing telegraph had loomed as the main competition to the Morse telegraph; the latter won out because the Morse code key was such a simple, cheap terminal. By 1876, however, ticker telegraphs were coming into use. In Britain the ABC telegraph was being promoted at that time. In the U.S. the Gold and Stock printing telegraph service was being extended by Western Union primarily as a business ticker. It was the threat to that service that led Western Union into brief competition with Bell in trying to develop a telephone system of its own.

The printing telegraph was a technology that was essentially defeated by the telephone. It turned out to be less satisfactory than the phone for an end-to-end point-to-point service. Its main drawback was the clumsy mechanical terminal required for printing.[42]

Had the phone not pre-empted the point-to-point market, progress undoubtedly would have been made in making the teletypewriter cheaper, smaller, and more reliable. But in the era before solid state electronics no one could see a way to make a printing terminal nearly as simple, durable, and economical as the telephone.

Had there been such a way, a human issue would have arisen of whether people preferred the ease of speaking or the advantages of a written record, or were willing to pay the extra cost for a dual mode system. Those issues, however, were not decisive and indeed hardly arose, for the economics were so unfavorable to the teletypewriter.

Today such human preferences are highly relevant, for computer terminals with a variety of forms of output, editing, and store and forward capabilities, and vastly changed costs and reliabilities, have upset the balance. Already by the 1920s a teletype was developed that was acceptable for some limited purposes such as those of news services and financial institutions. A switched teletypewriter service has been available in the U.S. since 1931.[43] Its use grew particularly in Europe where phone service was less good and more expensive than in the U.S. But computer networks reopen the competition in a wholly new way. In the period we are studying, however, the race was one-sided. The kind of telegraphy that *Punch* had in mind (cf. Section 1.1.2) never had a chance to develop once the telephone came along.

1.4.2 Plug in telephones will be used. (Type A)

Police systems (cf. Section 5.2.6.1) were offered a pocket telephone in 1912 that could be plugged into any call box.[44] Citizens too could carry it.

The argument was that they could carry it with them in neighborhoods where policemen were loath to patrol. Telephone linesmen carry phones that they can attach to the lines wherever they are.

The usefulness of a device that could go with the subscriber wherever he might be was thus obvious enough as soon as the phone lines were pervasive enough to cover a city reasonably well. That technical option was not developed, however, because it would have complicated the finances of the phone system. Billing would have been difficult, fraud easy, and with pre-electronic switching, finding a moving receiver also difficult.

It is only with land mobile radio telephony and now with CB transceivers that something approximating that device is coming into use. On an electronic switching system the billing of such a service also becomes practical. Indeed, long distance calls for some time have been billed to the subscriber's number from wherever he places the call. Only a sophisticated electronic switching system could do that for local calling at a tolerable cost.

Thus this forecast of portable phones failed, since though technically possible, they were economically impractical—the forecasters who focused on their usefulness failed to address these economic issues.

1.4.3 Phonographs.[45]

Several different uses were forecast for the phonograph as part of the telephone system.

1.4.3.1 Phonographs will be used as repeaters. (Type A)

Mechanical recording of a voice message and then amplified replay of it was an early idea for creating a repeater for long distance calling. This cumbersome, slow, and expensive idea was pre-empted by better methods. Yet Edison invented the phonograph with a repeater in mind, because he believed that few people would be able to afford their own telephone. His notion was that offices (such as telegraph offices) would use it to record spoken messages that would be transmitted by phone to a recorder at another office where the addressee could come to hear it.[46] Partly as a result of this misperception, it took Edison 15 years to realize the entertainment potential of the phonograph.

1.4.3.2 Phonographs will be used for long-distance multiplexing. (Type A)

One of the available ways to economize on the capital plant of either the telegraph or telephone system was to multiplex messages on the transmission lines. That was the purpose of the harmonic telegraph on which Bell was working when he invented the telephone.

Gen. Carty saw multiplexing as the main prospective use of the phonograph.

> The feature of the phonograph may become of greatest practical importance in telephony, by making it possible to carry on a number of conversations simultaneously over one circuit. . . .
>
> By this phonographic multiplex system, it would be possible to carry on one conversation in the ordinary way, then to have a phonograph transmitting a message at such speed that the vibrations impressed upon the line should be below the audible limit of the ear, and, consequently, having no effect on the original conversation. These slow vibrations could then be taken off upon a phonograph at the far end and reproduced at the normal rate.[47]

This approach, again, was pre-empted by more effective techniques.

1.4.3.3 Phonograph records will be sent as letters. (Type A)

Gen. Carty, among others, also predicted that people would start exchanging messages on phonograph records instead of written letters.[48] Before the wire recorder of 1905 the cumbersome wax discs were, however, hardly suitable for the purpose, but even today very mailable magnetic tapes and belts are little used for correspondence except in some developing countries where literacy is low. The often asserted preference of people for speaking over writing is apparently not dominant enough to cause letter writing to be replaced in this way. Senders would probably prefer to mail a voice recording; many letters start out in that form on a dictating machine. But the receiver's convenience is apparently better served by having a written letter which can be quickly scanned. So Gen. Carty's expectation is apparently not to be realized.

1.4.3.4 Phonograph records will be used as a storage medium in information retrieval systems. (Type A)

As soon as the phonograph appeared, the possible use of it for recording of phone messages was recognized. Gen. Carty wrote in 1901:

> One of the developments may be confidently expected is the phonographic dictionary, which shall be soon constructed that the busy correspondent, by simply touching a button, may have any word properly spelled, pronounced and defined . . .[49]

Not until the arival of solid state electonics could sophisticated selective information retrieval by coded button-pushing become cheap enough to be of interest. Today magnetic discs and prospectively the video disc are important information storage media, but electro-mechanical voice records were generally uneconomical as information storage devices. However, recording of some rudimentary information messages became a common adjunct to many phone systems. A good technological-economic analysis would have had to take account of the distinction between the economics of large and small message bases.

1.4.3.5 Telephone conversations will be recorded. (Type A)

The most important linkage of the telephone to recording machines has actually been for transcribing telephone conversations, as with telephone answering machines or for that matter in wire tapping. The use of recorders, however, has never reached levels that were sometimes anticipated. *Telephony* in 1901 predicted that the telephonograph "promises" to be one of the common conveniences of the coming century."[50]

When the first wire recorder was invented, *Telephony* saw it as primarily an enhancement for the telephone.

> This Danish miracle will legalize all transactions by telephone. By means of a wire it is connected with the ordinary telephone instrument, you ring up "Central," as usual, get your vis-a-vis, and go at him. Every word uttered by both speakers is recorded and can be carried to court.[51]

An unanticipated problem that has perhaps restricted the use of recordings is the man-hours required to listen to voice recordings.

1.4.4. Hands-free phones with loud-speakers will be used. (Type D)

Loud-speaker phones that allow one to talk while using both hands at work have been repeatedly marketed but have never acquired great popularity.[52] The familiar hand set is a more private device that does not interrupt everything else going on by filling the room with sound; it has apparently proved satisfactory. Some people expected otherwise; they thought the loud-speaker phone that produces a more naturalistic situation would be desired.

1.4.5 Transmission without wires.

In early telephone systems the bulk of the capital investment was in the wires. Any method of wireless telephony offered a great economy. The figures on early investment in copper wire have been presented in section 1.3.

Two approaches were considered for communicating without wires: use of light waves and use of radio waves.

1.4.5.1 Photophones will be used. (Type A)[53]

The first attempt at a wireless phone (which absorbed Bell in 1879–80) used light as a transmission medium, with a selenium recepter. However, until waveguides and optical fibers provided an entrapped light channel, the interferences in the natural environment precluded displacement of wire transmission by light. It is interesting to note that in April 1901, nine months before Marconi's transmission from Poldhu to Newfoundland but well after his 1896 patents, Carty, in his anonymous "Prophets Column" in the *Electrical Review,* evaluated radio waves versus light as possible means for long distance transmission and concluded that the prospects for light were better. He noted with interest the experiments showing the effect of sunspots on magnetic needles, but warned against promoters' talk of turning such phenomena to practical use for creating a trans-Atlantic voice cable. The ultimate possibilities he recognized:

> Ether is the Africa of Science, and not all of the gold and ivory of the Dark Continent would equal the rewards which await its successful explorers.[54]

But for his era he saw light as a more practical medium. He noted the success of Bell's photophone which enabled talk to be transmitted along a beam of light between two distant points not connected by wire.

> If it is possible to talk for a few hundred feet, why not for a mile, and if for a mile, who can say what the limit is?
>
> A system of telephony without wires seems one of the interesting possibilities and the distance on the earth through which it is possible to speak is theoretically limited only by the curvation of the earth . . . [55]

1.4.5.2. Radio telephony will be used (Type A)[16]

After the turn of the century, interest turned from light to the invisible Hertzian waves whose long distance transmission capacity Marconi had just demonstrated. From then until the 1920s, radio was not only a promise, but also a shadow on the horizon for AT&T. Vail and Carty came to realize that they had underestimated it and had allowed a new technology to emerge which could conceivably displace the wired phone system. In 1907, at the same time as de Forest's experiments were succeeding, Vail wrote to a London banker assuring him that "the difficulties of the wireless telegraph are as nothing compared with the difficulties in the way of the wireless telephone.

By 1909, however, Carty was asking for funds for research on a telephone repeater that, he said, "might put us in a position of control with regard to the art of wireless telephony, should it turn out to be a factor of importance." By 1911 Carty had convinced Vail that it was important.[57] While on balance they thought (correctly) that radio would not prove capable of providing transmission for a total national point-to-point message system, they were uncertain and later recognized that it had been a close call.

One result was a fundamental change to a more aggressive research and development policy, which we will discuss later under that heading (section 8.1). Here it is relevant to note the various assessments that were made of the possible uses of radio waves and of their potential impact on the phone system.

A. H. Griswold stated AT&T's basic assessment in an article in the *Bell Telephone Quarterly* in April, 1922.

1. Radio telephony was a supplement to and not a substitute for wire service;
2. Radio telephony would never replace universal wire service; and
3. It is evident that the cost of radio service would be excessive and that the character of the very limited service . . . would be far inferior."[58]

One use in which radio waves clearly had an economic advantage over the wired system was for one-to-many broadcasting, in which a single frequency band would be used simultaneously by very large numbers of listeners.[59] AT&T tried to get into that field too. That, however, is a story for our discussion of the telephone and the mass media, which comes later (section 4.7).

FOOTNOTES

[1] The letter, addressed "To the capitalists of the Electric Telephone Company," is reproduced in Pool, *The Social Impact of the Telephone*, pp. 156–7.

[2] The U.S. figures for number of telephones were:

1891	200,000
1894	291,000
1900	1,356,000
1902	2,370,000
1904	3,353,000
1908	6,484,000
1912	8,975,000
1914	10,046,000
1916	11,241,000
1920	13,329,000
1924	16,081,000
1928	19,341,000
1930	20,202,000

Among the many articles discussing this remarkable growth were: William Henry McDonough, "To Young Men Beginning Business: The Magic Telephone," *Saturday Evening Post,* June 14, 1902, in *Looking Forward*, Ray Brousseau, comp., New York: American Heritage Press, 1970, pp. 66-67; and also in *Telephony*, vol. 4, no. 2, August 1902, pp. 92-94 (with same title: "The Magic Telephone"). *Telephony*, August 1902, 4 (2), 92–94 with a projection for 1920 of over 15 million phones; Herbert Casson. The Telephone As It Is Today. *World's Work,* April 1910, 19, 12775–78; Casson. The Future of the Telephone. *World's Work,* May 1910 19, 12903–18, projecting to 1928; Henry Smith Williams. The Growth of the Telephone. *Science,* reprinted in *Hearst's Magazine,* October 1912, 22, 105–6; Burton J. Hendrick. Telephones for the Millions. *McClure's Magazine,* Oct. 1914, 44, 45–55, with a projection to 1930; William F. Ogburn. *The Social Effects of Avaiation.* Boston: Houghton Mifflin, 1940 pp. 137–39, projecting from 1940.

3 Annual Report, 1910.

4 From *ATT Financial Notes,* 1905.

5 Sidney H. Aronson. Bell's Electric Toy: What's the Use? The Sociology of Early Telephone Usage. In Pool, *The Social Impact of the Telephone*, p. 31.

6 Aronson, Bell's Electric Toy, p. 32.

7 A third "solution" proposed by some reformers was nationalization as a way to lower rates. European phone rates were indeed low but the systems worked badly and were small. Nonetheless, rates the poor could afford were often postulated as a political demand. For example, Rep. David J. Lewis of Maryland, speaking in the House of Representatives (March 4, 1915) proposed nationalization, a one-cent a call rate, and a phone in every home. (*Congressional Record,* vol. 52, part 6, Appendix, p. 847).

8 Cf. Aronson, Bell's Electric Toy, and also section 1.4.1.

9 Cf. discussion in Asa Briggs, The Pleasure Telephone: A Chapter in the Prehistory of the Media. In Pool. *The Social Impact of the Telephone.*

10 Colin Cherry. "The Telephone System: Creation of Mobility and Social Change. In Pool. *The Social Impact of the Telephone.*

11 Marion May Dilts. *The Telephone in a Changing World.* (New York: Longman's Green, 1941, p. 11.

12 Dilts, p. 16.

13 Cf. Jacques Attali and Yves Stourdze. The Birth of the Telephone and Economic Crisis: The Slow Death of the Monologue in French Society. In Pool *The Social Impact of the Telephone.* David Ralston. Impact of Society on Technology: The Development of the Telephone in the United States, Great Britain and France from 1876 to 1914 (unpublished manuscript) (no date).

14 Cf. Charles R. Perry. In Pool. *The Social Impact of the Telephone;* Ralston. Impact of Society on Technology. The British Experience 1876–1912: The Impact of the Telephone During the Years of Delay.

15 Cf. Robert V. Bruce, *Bell:Alexander Graham Bell and the Conquest of Solitude.* Boston: Little Brown, 1973, p. 216.

16 Cf. Cherry, The Telephone System, p. 115, which notes the importance of the conceptual model provided by the somewhat different telegraph exchanges. A telegraph exchange functioned in Philadelphia as early as 1867. The first one goes back to 1837. Cf. also Aronson, *Bell's Electric Toy;* John E. Kingsbury. *The Telephone and Telephone Exchanges.* New York; 1972, p. 74.

[17]Arthur Vaughen Abbott. Bulletin of the University of Wisconsin, Engineering Series, 1894, *1* (4), 70.

[18]On the policy "that telephones should be leased and never sold except for export" see Hubbard memor to Bell, Feb. 28, 1879 in *Walker Report,* Federal Communications Commission, vol. 1, Appendix A.

[19] Fred de Laud. Telephone Service: The Relative Cost to the User. *Electrical Engineering,* 1895 5, 337–346.

[20] Bruce, *Bell,* p. 210.

[21] Aronson, "Bell's Electric Toy, p. 21

[22] Tenth Annual Report; Cf. Theodore N. Vail. Public Utilities and Public Policies. *Atlantic Monthly,* March 1913, *111,* 315–9; Sydney Brooks. Politics of American Business. *North American Review,* May 1911, *93,* 713.

[23] The 1876 patent clearly specified a device for providing both telephone and telegraph service. The two "T's" in the company's initials were not inadvertant. The Bell System's first long distance line in 1879 was for telegraph service.

[24] Cf. The Passing of the Telephone Girl. *Harpers Weekly,* Sept. 18, 1909, *53,* 37, on Germany.

[25] Dilts, *The Telephone in a Changing World;* p. 28. CF. ATT Annual Report, 1904.

[26] I.W. Aitkin. Automatic Telephone Exchange Systems. *Science,* American Supplement, Jan. 13, 1912, *73,* 20–22.

[27] Pool. *The Social Impact of the Telephone,* p. 156.

[28] Dilts. *The Telephone in a Changing World.*

[29] Quoted in R.B. Hill. Some Early Telephone Prophecies. *Bell Telephone Quarterly,* April 1936, *15* (2), 123.

[30] Casson. The Telephone As It Is Today, p. 12775. Vail understood the strategic advantage of controlling the long lines. From 1881 until 1897 the company issued a national telephone directory. Eventually it had to be regretfully abandoned, for it became too big.

[31] Roger Burlingame. *Engines of Democracy.* New York: C. Scribner, 1940, pp. 118f.

[32] Burlingame, *Engines of Democracy,* p. 118–119.

[33] Casson. The Telephone As It Is Today, p. 12776. Casson's tale simplifies; the Boston to New York Line was not an instant success. It was initially noisy and had the severe problems that all long distance lines did until adequate repeaters were developed. However, its very existence was a triumph, and quality of service gradually improved.

[34] The Immediate Future of the Long-distance Telephone in *Current Literature,* May 1911, *50,* no author 504, reports the laying of an experimental submarine telephone cable between France and England. Conversations between London and the whole European continent are, it says, now possible, and conversations are now possible over up to 1700 miles of cable. The article looks forward to the time, far in the future, when the whole globe will be linked together.

[35] Stephen Dizard. *Industrial Development of the Telephone,* p. 3. (unpublished manuscript)

[36] AT&T, Annual Report, 1908, p. 22.

[37] It is worth noting that similar points can be made about Marconi and the history of wireless telegraphy. After Hertzian waves were discovered in 1888, a number of

scientists recognized that they could be used, in the way that electrical transmissions over wires were already being used, for communications devices. Marconi's important insight, aside from his entrepreneurial ones, was the conviction, successfully demonstrated by him, that those waves could go a long way. His great triumph was his trans-Atlantic transmission in 1901.

[38] Often optimistic forecasts eventually came true as technical and economic difficulties were overcome, but more slowly than the forecaster expected. In January 1901 Edward E. Clement heralded the new century with an article on Twenteith Century Possibilities, (*Telephony*, Jan. 1901, p. 5). He not only forecast long distance service, but that it would be without "heavy special trunk lines" and that callers could talk not only within their city, but among cities "without heavy expense or extra trouble." The trouble was eliminated only in recent decades with direct distance dialing; distance insensitivity of cost is still not quite here, but is likely to be with us by the end of the century, about which Clement was writing.

[39] Hill. Some Early Telephone Prophecies, p. 123.

[40] Hill. Some Early Telephone Prophecies, pp. 125–6. H.G. Wells in his 1902 book *Anticipations,* which forecasts the nature of life in the 20th century, notes the possibility of telecommunicating to "any part of the world."

[41] John J. Carty, *Electrical Engineering,* 1891, *1*, 160. W. Clyde Jones made the same forecast in the same journal, (The Evolution of the Telephone, 1893, p. 8.)

[42] For that reason, new devices such as facsimile were sometimes forecast as means for evading that problem, e.g., Jones, The Evolution of the Telephone, p. 8 on the telautograph (1893); See also Aronson, Bell's Electric Toy, quoting E. A. Marland, *Early Electrical Communication,* (London: Abelard-Schuman, 1964), p. 185.

[43] An initial attempt at offering that kind of service was made by the Berlin phone company in 1903. "Berlin Teletyping Central Station" *Telephony* 8, No. 1, July, 1904, p. 36.

[44] A Pocket Telephone. *Literary Digest,* March 30, 1912, *44*, p. 639.

[45] See also Section 8.1.1.

[46] Daniel Boorstein. *The Americans: The Democratic Experience.* New York: Random House, 1973, p. 379.

[47] Carty. Prohets Column. *Electrical Review, 19* (5), 66, Sept. 26, 1891.

[48] Carty, Prophets Column. *Electrical Review, 19* (1), 2, Aug. 29, 1891.

[49] Carty. The Prophet's Column. *Electrical Review, 18,* (7), 98. April 11, 1891.

[50] The Telephonograph. *Telephony,* Feb. 1901, *1* (2) 29. See also The Telephonograph. *Science,* vol. 12 (N.S.) Nov. 23, 1900, *12* (308), 812–3; TheTelephone That Remembers, *Telephony,* 1904, *8* (1), 69.

[51] New Recording Telephone. *Telephony,* Sept. 1905, *10* (3), 196. On admissability of telephone conversations in evidence, see Section 4.3.2.

[52] E.g. the Weilaphone described in Improving Telephone Service. *American Architecture,* Dec. 18, 1918, *114*, 753; Clement, Twentieth Century Possibilities.

[53] Cf., section 8.1.4.

[54] Carty. Prophets Column. *Electrical Review, April 11, 1891, 18* (7), 98; For an example of speculation about communication by Hertzian waves see Clement, Twentieth Century Possibilities.

[55] Carty. Prophets Column. *Electrical Review. April 25, 1891, 18* (9), 121.

[56] Cf., sections 4.7.2.3. and 8.1.4.

[57] N.R. Danielson. *AT&T: The Story of Industrial Conquest.* New York: Vanguard, 1939, pp. 104f. Cf. John Brooks. *Telephone.* New York: Harper and Row, 1976, p. 140. Cf. Dizard, *Business Planning and Telephone Research, 1875–1925* (unpublished manuscript).

[58] A.H. Griswold, The Radio Telephone Situation. *Bell Telephone Quarterly,* April 1922, 2, 4–7.

[59] Griswold's assessment noted that the Bell system was trying broadcasting in New York, and that if commercially successful this would spread, and stations could be networked by the long lines telephone plant.

2

Effects of the
Telephone on Patterns
of Human Settlement

2.1 Urban ecology.

2.1.1 The telephone fosters the separation of plant and office. (Type A)

In the mid-19th century, if one walked up to one of the big red brick sheds along the rivers of the North East which housed most American factories, one would have found the offices of the company and its president at the front of the building with the production plant behind. By the 1920s, however, one would have found most corporate headquarters located in Manhattan or in the downtowns of Pittsburgh, Cleveland, Chicago, or some other metropolis and the factories on the outskirts or in smaller manufacturing towns.

Peter Cowan in his book, *The Office,* notes that in New York "a cluster of central offices . . . began to accumulate in the late 1880's or early 1890's . . . In London . . . the building of offices got under way during the first part of the century." (p. 29.) Cowan attributes the character of office activity to three inventions: the telegraph, the typewriter, and the telephone, especially the last two.[1] The company president located himself at the place where most of his most critical communications took place. Before the telephone he had to be near the production line to give his instructions about the quantities, pace, and process of production. Once the telephone network existed, however, he could convey those authoritative commands to his employees at the plant and locate himself at the place where the much more uncertain bargaining with customers, bankers, and suppliers took place.

Thus at the turn of the century the downtowns of American cities changed from loft areas and manufacturing centers to concentrations of white collar workers in office buildings.

We found no evidence of the 19th century anticipations of this evolution, though Bell and the earliest telephone entrepreneurs recognized that perhaps the prime customers for their service were businessmen who would put a pair of phones in their plant and store, or plant and warehouse, or separate plants if

41

there was more than one, or plant or store and owner's residence.[2] They did not speculate, however, on the long run effects which that might have on urban ecology. After the turn of the century, contemporaries were well aware of what was happening. Herbert Casson wrote in 1911, "The foreman of a Pittsburgh coal company may now stand in his subterranean office and talk to the president of the Steel Trust, who sits on the twenty-first floor of a New York skyscraper."[3]

While quantitatively the separation of corporate offices from manufacturing plants was the most important part of the process of creating a commercial downtown, the same sort of thing was happening in other enterprises besides industry. Before the availability of the telephone, doctors, for example, had to live near their offices to be readily available when needed; typically, in fact, the office was in the doctor's home. The telephone allowed many doctors to separate home and office, and to put the office where it was convenient for the patients to come.[4]

2.1.2 The telephone fosters the growth of downtowns. (Type B)

The process of agglomeration of commercial and professional activities towards a common location led to the growth of the downtowns of American cities. So did a number of the other processes about to be discussed in this section.

2.1.3 The telephone encourages scattering of particular business districts. (Type B)[5]

Before the telephone, businessmen needed to locate close to their business contacts. Every city had a furrier's neighborhood, a hatter's neighborhood, a wool neighborhood, a fishmarket, an egg market, a financial district, a shipper's district, and many others. Businessmen would pay mightily for an office within the few blocks where their trade was centered; their way of doing business was to walk up and down the block and drop in to the places from which one might buy or to whom one might sell. For lunch or coffee, one might drop in to the corner restaurant or tavern where one's colleagues congregated.

Once the telephone was available, businesses could move to cheaper quarters and still keep in touch. A firm could move outwards, as many businesses did, or move up to the 10th or 20th story of one of the new tall buildings. Instead of an urban pattern of a checkerboard of different specialized neighborhoods, the new urban pattern entailed a large downtown containing a miscellany of commercial and marketing activities that needed to be accessible to a variety of clients and customers, a growing set of satellite downtowns, for more convenient shopping and services, and the exiling of those activities that needed little outside contact (like manufacture) to peripheral locations.

2.1.4 The telephone favors the growth of skyscrapers. (Type B)

Recognition of how the telephone contributed to a revolution in modern architecture, namely the creation of skyscrapers, appears as early as 1902 in an article in *Telephony*.[6] General Carty used the same arguments in 1908.

> It may sound ridiculous to say that Bell and his successors were the fathers of modern commercial architecture—of the skyscraper. But wait a minute. Take the Singer Building, the Flatiron, the Broad Exchange, the Trinity, or any of the giant office buildings. How many messages do you suppose go in and out of those buildings every day. Suppose there was no telephone and every message had to be carried by a personal messenger. How much room do you think the necessary elevators would leave for offices? Such structures would be an economic impossibility.[7]

The pre-history of the skyscraper begins with the elevator in the 1850s; the first Otis elevator was installed in a New York City store in 1857, and with adaption to electric power in the 1880s, the device came into general use.[8] "The need to rebuild Chicago after the 1871 fire, rapid growth, and rising land values encouraged experimentation in construction." In 1884 Jenney erected a 10 story building with a steel skeleton as a frame, the 57 storied Woolworth Building was opened in 1913; "By 1929 American cities had 377 skyscrapers of more than twenty stories."[9]

There were several ways in which the telephone contributed to that development. We have already noted that human messengers would have required too many elevators at the core of the building to make it economic. Furthermore, telephones were useful in skyscraper construction; the superintendent on the ground could use a phone to keep in touch with the workers on the scaffolding. As the building went up, a line was dropped from the upper girders to the ground.

2.1.5 The telephone will lead to the growth of suburbs and to urban sprawl. (Type B)[10]

As the telephone broke down old business neighborhoods and made it possible to move to cheaper quarters, the telephone/tall-building combination offered an option of moving up instead of moving out. One of our initial impressions when we began this study was that the automobile and the telephone were jointly responsible for the vast growth of American suburbia and exurbia, and for the phenomenon of urban sprawl. There is some truth to that, even though everything we have said so far seems to point to the reverse proposition that the telephone made possible the skyscraper and increased the congestion downtown. Paradoxically, both propositions are true, but to different degrees in different periods. The impact of the phone today and its net impact 70 years ago are almost reverse.

The movement out to residential suburbs began in the decade before the invention of the telephone and thus long before the automobile. The streetcar was the key at the beginning.[11] Today streetcars have vanished; automobiles and telephones now make it possible for metropolitan regions to spread over thousands of square miles.[12]

There were two options open to urban enterprises and residents as neighborhoods broke up, the economics of location changed, and cities grew. One was to move up into the new tall buildings, the other was to move out from the center. Today our attention is focused on the dramatic movement outward, and the resulting urban sprawl. We have tended to lose sight of the duality of the movement; the skyscraper slowed the spread. It helped keep many people downtown and intensified the downtown congestion. Contemporary observers noted this, but in recent decades we have tended to forget it. Burlingame, for example, said in 1940:

> It is evident that the skyscraper and all the vertical congestion of city business centers would have been impossible without the telephone. Whether, in the future, with its new capacities, it will move to destroy the city it helped to build is a question for prophets rather than historians.[13]

He sensed that things were changing. The flight from downtown was already perceptible enough for him to note it, but as a qualification to his description of the process of concentration; both processes have taken place at once throughout the era of the telephone. The telephone is a facilitator used by people with opposite purposes. (Cf. Section 5.2.6.2 for another example of this point.)

2.1.6 The telephone will help create megalopolises.
(Type B)

As Jean Gottmann points out, the telephone has favored a movement toward megalopolis, not antipolis.[14] A megalopolis such as Bos-Wash is not, he stresses, an undifferentiated sprawl of medium density settlement. It is a highly differentiated structure with numerous centers and subcenters having complex interrelations. Other commentators have seen the concept of a megalopolis as meaning the destruction of the great urban cultural centers; Gottman disagrees. A megalopolis, as he describes it, is an enlarged and more complex system of differentiation.

In 1902 H.G. Wells forecast centrifugal forces on cities that may lead "to the complete reduction of all our present congestions."[15] A pedestrian city, he said, "is inexorably limited by a radius of about four miles, and a horse-using city may grow out to seven or eight." With street railways the modern city thrusts "out arms along every available railway line."

> It follows that the available area of a city which can offer a cheap suburban journey of thirty miles an hour is a circle with a radius of thirty miles. . . . But thirty miles is only a very moderate estimate of speed. . . . I think, that the available area . . . will have a radius of over one hundred miles. . . . Indeed, it is not too much to say . . . that the vast stretch of country from Washington to Albany will be all of it "available" to the active citizen of New York and Philadelphia.[16]

He anticipates "that New York, Philadelphia, and Chicago will probably, and Hankow almost certainly, reach forty millions." The telephone was one factor Wells listed as fostering this development,[17] for he believed that there is no reason "why a telephone call from any point in such a small country as England to any other should cost more than a post-card."[18] Yet Wells, like Gottmann later, emphasizes that urban sprawl does not mean uniformity of density. Shopping and entertainment centers will continue to make downtowns, while people in some occupations will prefer to move out to the country and work by phone from home.[19]

The *Scientific American* article of 1914 called "Action at a Distance"[20] has similar themes, but with special stress on the picture phone as likely to make dispersion possible. "It is evident," it starts out, "that something will soon have to be done to check the congestion" of the city. "The fundamental difficulty . . . seems to be that it is necessary for individuals to come into close proximity to each other if they are to transact business." The telephone and picturephone, it is argued, will change all that.

2.1.7 The telephone, at one stage, fosters stabilization and differentiation of neighborhoods. (Type B)

We noted above how the telephone had contributed to the break-up of single-trade neighborhoods. But in this, as in so many ways with the telephone, the instrument also had a dual effect, fostering opposite tendencies at different times and in different ways. It tended at an early stage of its development to encourage the stablization of "good" neighborhoods and business districts and their separation from areas of decay.

Phone entrepreneurs, when they were getting started, like cable television entrepreneurs today, could not afford to wire the whole city fully and at once. They preferred to lay their lines where they could expect to recruit many subscribers, i.e., in affluent or business districts. The concentration of potential subscribers within an area was advantageous to the utility before it had achieved universal coverage.

2.1.7.1 Telephone and other utility companies support zoning. (Type A)

Shifting and deteriorating neighborhoods were not good for business. Zoning of a city helped in planning for future services, so the phone companies (along with other utilities) became supporters of the zoning movement.[21] The Department of Commerce's zoning primer of 1923 states: "expensive public services . . . are maintained at great waste in order to get through the blighted districts to the more distant and fashionable locations."[22]

With an insensitivity that reflects the times and would be unthinkable today, Smith and Campbell said:

> It should not be taken for granted that this satisfies the requirements unless there is at least one telephone for every eight inhabitants in an average American city, in which practically everyone is white. Where a large portion of the population belongs to the negro race, or a considerable portion of the population is made up of very poor workers in factories, the requirements will be less. In some cities one telephone to fifteen inhabitants is all that can be expected.[23]

Zoning, along with other efforts at urban planning, became popular around the turn of the century. After the Chicago fire in 1871 building codes were enacted (around 1890) with explicit provisions for fireproofing.[24] Codes dealt with allowable building heights and the location of tall buildings in the city. The idea of a planned city was contained in such books as Robinson's *Improvement of Towns and Cities*[25] and Ebenezer Howard's *Garden Cities of Tomorrow*,[26] first published in 1898. Zoning actually began in New York in 1916.

While the phone company supported the zoning movement in general, on one point it was at odds with the urban planners. Zoning was often used to set height limits, restricting the construction of tall buildings. Such buildings, however, were heavy telephone users. The phone companies opposed height limitations.

2.1.7.2 Telephone companies provide much of the information for urban planning. (Type A)

In the crucial second decade of the century, phone companies were one of the main sources of information for the new urban plans. They collected large amounts of neighborhood data on the population trends in the city, its businesses, and its neighborhoods; the telephone was used as a device for conducting the research.

> The most direct means of approaching citizens on the planning issue was reported in Los Angeles where a battery of phone girls called everyone in the city to secure reactions, while mailing an explanatory folder.[27]

2.1.7.3 The telephone system requires the publication of directories. (Type A)

In the 19th century, well before the invention of the telephone, directories of cities were being published. From the beginning of switched telephone systems it was recognized as important to give subscribers a list of other subscribers. This list was particularly important if subscribers were to be called by number. These listings were originally printed on a card to hang by the phone. By 1897 the national phone directory was a big book, too big in fact to be economic to distribute free to subscribers so the Bell System retreated to publishing and giving out separate local phone books, even though this restriction was a blow to the promotion of toll service.

As telephones became universal among businesses and later, fairly universal among the public, the phone book became the most widely used city directory. It had to be issued often to keep with the growth of the system; it was available everywhere; and it was free. The classified version of the directory was particularly useful for many business purposes. It became the basis for much canvassing and sampling. It incidentally impacted the business of other city directories which had to be sold in competition with the free phone book, but accordingly it forced them to provide more information if they were to survive. For the ordinary citizen the telephone book became the standard means not only to finding phone numbers, but also of finding mailing addresses and business locations.[28]

2.1.7.4 Zoning tends to increase social segregation. (Type B)

A long run effect of zoning that has caused it to be a far less popular panacea among reformers today than it was in the years before World War I, is to sharpen the lines of social segregation in cities. Neighborhoods of the rich are protected for the rich. That was understood at the time, but not then regarded as evil. The New York zoning report wrote that "one purpose of districting regulations is to strengthen and supplement the natural trend toward segregation." Hubbard and Hubbard wrote in 1929 that by distinguishing single family residences from multiple dwellings, zoning has removed "obstacles from an open statement of a socially important classification."[29]

2.1.8 The telephone facilitates the coordination of the urban system. (Type B)

When the telephone was 50 years old, Arthur Pound, in an anniversary volume,[30] used a familar theme, noting how the life of a city could grind down to a crawl if the phones all suddenly stopped working. The trains, the produce dealers, the hospitals would all be in trouble.

Later in this inventory we shall deal with the use of the telephone for the logistics and coordination of a number of special city functions such as police work, fire fighting, and transportation. But the point may be generalized. It is hard to conceive of a metropolis running its myriad functions well without extensive use of the telephone. Some cities do function with much less use of the phone than we in the United States take for granted. Peking, Calcutta, and Moscow are large cities with very limited telephone service by our standards, yet they function. But it need hardly be doubted that the way they function is severely restricted due to limited use of the telephone and would suffer much more were there no phones at all.

2.1.9 The change of independent villages into satellites of cities is fostered by the telephone. (Type B)

· Several developments in the first fifteen years of the 20th century undermined the autonomy of small towns and villages and increased commercial concentration in larger centers, bypassing the nearby village. Four of these developments were parcel post, rural free delivery, the automobile, and the telephone. All of these led farmers to do their banking, buying, and selling in larger, more remote centers rather than at the nearest rural village, and indeed led villagers to take their trade to better stocked, more developed centers away from home. Rural free delivery favored the growth of mail order business and reduced the need for farmers to come to the local post office. Parcel post was established by Congress in 1912 over the vigorous opposition of the small town merchants who saw it as a subsidy to Sears Roebuck and as destroying the small-town backbone of American democracy.[31] The significance of the automobile is obvious. So, to some degree, is the impact of the telephone. Many early rural phone systems were just tiny local networks which would have fostered village communication only. But by the second decade of this century such systems were being rapidly interconnected with the national network. We will note in Section 2.2.1 the many advantages the farmer got from being able to telephone to the markets and services of the urban centers, cutting down his dependence on the middleman in the village.

2.2 Rural Life.

A priori reasoning about the diffusion of the telephone in rural areas can lead to two opposite conjectures. Given the isolation of farmers and the profound change the telephone could make in their lives, one might expect that telephones would have spread faster in rural than in urban areas. Given the cost of the miles of wire needed to reach isolated farmsteads, one might expect that telephone service would come more slowly and later to rural than to urban areas. Both assessments are valid and the result is an unstable equilibrium. Which way it comes out at any time or place depends upon a variety of circumstances concerning both demand and supply.

2.2.1 The telephone will be particularly attractive and valuable to farmers. (Type A)

With a telephone in the house, a buggy in the barn, and a rural mail box at the gate, the problem of how to keep the boys and girls on the farm is solved,[32]

said a 1905 article in *Telephony,* one of many praising the phone for its usefulness to farmers.

About every six months *Telphony* would run such a paean to the telephone and how it had transformed farm life from a desperate struggle with loneliness and hardship into a tolerable career.[33] The main themes were:

2.2.1.1 The telephone will abolish loneliness, particularly for the farmer's wife. (Type B)

A city woman who moved to the country wrote an article in 1912, called "The Teeming Country", denying the notion of rural loneliness, mostly because of the telephone.

> Now when I open the telephone to see if the line is busy, and catch this scrap of conversation, ". . . but they do get so black when they're old and Joel says it'll be three weeks before they're big enough to dig," I say with as spontaneous an impulse as though I had never lived in a lonely stone canyon of a street: "Oh Miss Maria, if you'll put a few drops of lemon juice in the water you boil them in, they'll be as white and mealy as new ones."
>
> There is no pause of horrified resentment at my instrusion. A friendly voice says, "That you, Mrs. F---? Much obliged. I'll try it. Don't forget 'bout th' church supper tonight!"[34]

The party line was often used for group chatter, in the fashion of CB radio today.

2.2.1.2 The telephone will provide security despite isolation. (Type A)

Hendrick in 1914 wrote:

> Many a lonely farmer's wife or daughter, on the approach of a suspicious-looking character, has rushed to the telephone and called up the neighbors; so that now tramps notoriously avoid houses that shelter the protecting wires.[35]

In the section on the telephone in emergencies (5), we shall discuss the telephone and fire, crime, and illness. Each of these uses of the phone appears also in the discussion of farm telephones, with the security problems accentuated by the extra dimension of remoteness. There are stories of a farmer's barn saved from fire, or of his child's life saved because of the speed with which help could be called.

2.2.1.3 The telephone will bring prompt weather warnings. (Type A)[36]

A 1905 article in *Telephony* predicted that "almost every American Farmer will receive the daily weather bulletin in his home before noon of the day it is issued."[37] Like any of the other functions we are noting here, this one was partly taken over by the radio after the mid 1920s, but in the previous 15 years the telephone was for the farmer what radio became. It warned him of approaching storms or cold snaps,[38] and indeed it still does.

2.2.1.4 The telephone is useful for rural community organization. (Type A)

In many places, every evening at about 7:00 the farmers on a party line would pick up their phones and have a community meeting[39] The main news of the day would be read. Problems would be discussed and plans laid for joint activity.[40] Indeed setting up the phone system itself was often a cooperative activity.

2.2.1.5 The telephone enables farmers to get prompt and accurate market information. (Type A)

"Through the telephone," wrote Wilbur Wheeler Bassett,

> it seems inevitable that the farmer will assume a new economic position. Keeping in touch with the market, he is able to dispose of produce directly to the city dealer or to the consumer without the assistance of any middlemen. Fluctuations in the market will be felt immediately by the producer, and he will be able to prevent any advantage being taken of him. He may talk to his town buyer and to his city broker the same hour and sell his produce at the top of the market.[41]

He illustrated his point by a story of phoneless broomcorn growers in southern Illinois who were selling their product for $60 a ton when the market price had risen to four times that, while farmers who had phones got the market price.[42]

As in innumerable other magazine articles, Burton Hendrick reports how a farmer in Vermont avoided getting too low a price for his apples by calling the market.

> This one telephone conversation netted him $250. . . . In the old days the Kansas farmer used to carry his grain into market by wagon. He would usually hang about all day dickering with middlemen. These agile gentlemen always had him at a disadvantage. Unless he disposed of his load that day, he either had to carry it back to the farm, or stay in town, sometimes for several days, until he had disposed of it. Now he sells his product by wire, and carts it to market only when sold.[43]

A 1906 *Telephony* article claimed that by enabling farmers to take advantage of fluctuations in the grain and livestock markets, the phone "added many a dollar to the yearly profit. The price of farm lands has increased wherever rural lines have been extended."[44]

A similar point was made with the opposite value judgment in France in 1908. Paris papers blamed the farmers' use of the telephone for the rise in the price of meat in the city.[45]

2.2.1.6 The rural operator provides many community services. (Type A)

The helpful and all knowing rural operator is the heroine of both fiction and popular articles. She kept track of the movements and needs of her customers. The city-born author of "The Teeming Country"[46] recalls her first rural phone call; she asked for the grocer and the operator informed her he was home eating dinner.

Operators frequently provided information services, such as weather reports, times of meetings, latest news, etc.[47]

2.2.2 The telephone will stem the flight from the farms. (Type B)

From all the above-listed benefits that the phone would bring to rural life the conclusion was sometimes drawn, as above (2.2.1) that the migration off the land to the cities would stop.[48]

Could a prediction be more wrong! In 1905, 34% of the American work force were farmers. By now it is 3%.

But in another light perhaps the analysis is not so wrong. Did the telephone, along with the automobile, electricity, radio, and television, stem the pace of a movement that was largely determined by agricultural economics? The techniques of production, wages on the farm and in the city, and the price of the product may be what determines how many farmers are farming. Today however, with cars and paved roads most farmers could live in town and commute to the fields. If many farmers still prefer to live on their farmsteads how much is that due to the fact that in his farm home he can now have electric lights, a freezer, a TV, a telephone, and virtually any other convenience of urban life. Perhaps *ceteris paribus* the telephone has stemmed the flight from the farm even if it has not stopped it; there is no way we can be sure.

2.2.3 The spread of telephones in the countryside.

From all the considerations just noted it is clear that the telephone had much to offer farmers, but as we have already noted, getting service to them could be expensive and difficult. This balance led to two pairs of opposed propositions that represented the views of major contenders in the telephone business during the first two decades of this century.

The contradictory conclusions that stemmed from these opposing considerations can be stated in two pairs of propositions, one pair representing the philosophy of the Bell System at that time, the other pair representing the philosophy of the independents. On the matter of the speed of phone system penetration in the countryside, the Bell System was bearish, concentrating its efforts in the main metropolitan centers. The independents bet on a rural market. On the matter of what kind of phone system a rural area needed, the Bell System insisted on a high quality interconnected phone system everywhere, while many independents settled for second class, low cost systems limited to the local exchange area.

2.2.3.1   Speed of penetration.

2.2.3.1.1   The telephone will spread in the countryside fast.
(Type A)

2.2.3.1.2   The telephone will spread in the countryside slowly.
(Type A)

In fact, the speed of diffusion of the telephone in the countryside shows interesting reversals. Until Bell patents expired in 1893, the system used its limited capital to grow, fanning out from the network already established, i.e., mainly spreading out from the northeast and mainly in urban areas. The period from 1894 was one of rapid growth and competition as independents sought to strike roots, particularly in the western and rural areas that had not yet been pre-empted. In prosperous rural areas the growth of farm telephones was astonishing. Early in the century Iowa led the nation in penetration. Between 1902 and 1907 rural phones increased from 267,000 to 1,465,000.[49] In 1907, 160,000 out of 220,000 farms in Iowa (73%) had telephones.[50]

On the other hand, in poor rural areas, as in parts of the south, telephone penetration remained very low.

But the spread of farm telephones peaked in the 1920's.[51] There were more telephones on farms in 1920 than in 1940![52] There are a number of hidden facts behind that extraordinary figure. In the first place there was was the Depression. Telephone growth in general was checked in the thirties; but except on farms there was no such dramatic decline as a fall below the 1920 level. The second explanation is the flight from the farms; the number of farms declined from 6,517,500 in 1920 to 6,349,800 in 1940.[53] A third factor was the arrival of radio in the 1920s; having a telephone became less important to farmers once they could learn about the weather, market prices, and the world from the radio.

So even though there had been a "veritable telephone crusade among the farmers of the Middle West"[54] in the 1910s, a plateau had been reached and the poorer, more isolated farmers remained the last major population group without telephone service, until Rural Electrification Administration loans at 2% became available in 1949 for rural telephone cooperatives.

In Germany, phones were first introduced in 1877 by Bismark to serve rural villages that could not afford a telegraph operator, but after 1880 most phone growth there was urban.

2.2.3.2   Character of the rural phone system.

2.2.3.2.1   Rural areas need a special kind of low-cost phone system. (Type A)

2.2.3.2.2   Rural areas need a standard interconnected phone system. (Type A)

In the U.S. one of the secrets of the remarkable rural telephone growth of the first two decades of the century (which brought rural penetration rates up to and beyond urban rates in many states) was that the systems installed were extremely simple and cheap. The rural independents did not maintain the quality standards insisted upon by the Bell System.[55] Such primitive systems used party lines; the transmission was sometimes carried by fence wires; the poles and wires were often strung and maintained by the farmers themselves. In some villages the functions of the operator were performed by a housewife or storekeeper alongside of their regular duties. What was installed was in effect a large intercom, and at first mostly not interconnected with other systems, so the only calls that could be made were within the system.[56]

At issue during this period was the question of whether that was all that farmers needed or could pay for. Between such a system and a professionally manned, interconnected, amortized system the cost difference was an order of magnitude. It will be recalled that many systems' costs went up combinatorially with size (Section 1.2.1). So one could make a case that the marginal cost for going from a rudimentary mutual system to becoming a part of the national telephone network was not worth it to the farmer—and many small phone systems made that case.

In the end, however, Theodore Vail's philosophy and the Bell System won out. He argued that the future lay with high quality, therefore high cost, interconnected and properly amortized systems. And so it turned out. Rural systems, if well organized, grew and soon the customers demanded to be interconnected at least with the nearby market cities, and once the system had such capability, why not with the national network? So maturity eventually resulted in the merger of the interconnected rural systems into the Bell System.[57]

One further factor pushing in that direction was the electrification of the country. Poorly designed, low cost systems, particularly those with ground return, were prone to electrical interference. They could function reasonably when they did not run into strong electrical currents, but that became a rare situation.

Nonetheless, the burst of autonomous local telephone activity by rural co-ops and entrepreneurs played an important transitional role in the development of the American telephone system.[58] Nothing like that happened in most European countries, where the government regarded telephone development as their monopoly and did not give freedom to local initiatives.

2.2.4 The telephone will reduce the difference between rural and urban life. (Type C)

A quarter of a century before the invention of the telephone, Karl Marx forecast that as part of the revolution he anticipated, industrial development would end the separation of society's rural and urban sectors. The specific impacts of the telephone that we have just noted go in that direction, making life on the farm more urbane and less isolated from town. As Basset put it: "The telephone . . . destroys the barrier between city and country. Henceforth the country is but a vast suburb."[59]

FOOTNOTES

[1] Peter Cowan. *The Office.* New York; American Elsevier, 1969, p. 30.

[2] The first long-distance line from Boston to Lowell was successful partially because factory owners in Boston wished to talk to their plants in Lowell.

[3] Herbert Casson. The Social Value of the Telephone. *The Independent,* Oct. 26, 1911, *71*, 901.

[4] Telephone and Doctor, *Literary Digest,* May 18, 1912, *44*, 1037. Cf. Section 5.2.7.4. 5.2.7.4.

[5] See Jean Gottmann. Megalopolis and Antipolis: The Telephone and the Structure of the City. In Pool, *The Social Impact of the Telephone;* Ronald Abler. The Telephone and the Evolution of the American Metropolitan System. In Pool; J. Allen Moyer. Urban Growth and the Development of the Telephone: Some Relationships at the Turn of the Century. In Pool.

[6] Application of the Modern Telephone. *Telephony,* Aug. 1902, *4* (2), 94–95.

[7] In John Kimberly Mumford. This Land of Opportunity, The Nerve Center of Business. *Harper's Weekly,* August 1, 1908, *52* 23.

[8] Charles N. Glaab and A. Theodore Brown. *A History of Urban America.* New York: Macmillian, 1967, pp. 144–5.

9 Glaab and Brown. *A History of Urban America,* p. 280.

10 Cf. Section 9.2.

11 Cf. Moyer. Urban Growth and the Development of the Telephone. In Pool, op. cit; S. B. Warner, Jr., *Streetcar Suburbs.* Cambridge: Harvard University Press, 1962.

12 Early relevant discussions of suburbanization include: Frederick A.C. Perrine, Electrical Engineering and Social Reform *Electrical Engineering,* 1894, *3* (2) 39 (stressing electric street cars); Action at a Distance, *Scientific American* Supplement No. 1985, 17, 1914, *77,* 39 (stressing phone and future picturephone); and Wells, *Anticipations.*

13 Burlingame. *Engines of Democracy,* p. 96; cf. Arthur Page, Social Aspects of Communication Development. In Page (Ed.) *Modern Communication.* Boston: Houghton Mifflin, 1932. He notes the relation of the phone to both the skyscraper and suburb, and says it "allows us to congregate where we wish to" (p. 20).

14 Gottmann. Megalopolis and Antipolis; Gottmann.

15 Wells. *Anticipations,* p. 51,

16 Wells. *Anticipations,* pp. 52–53.

17 Wells. *Anticipations,* p. 65.

18 Wells. *Anticipations,* p. 58.

19 Wells. *Anticipations,* p. 66.

20 Action at a Distance, *Scientific American* Supplement 1985, Jan. 17, 1914, *77,* p. 39.

21 Telephone, electric light, gas, and trolley companies report that zoning is making it possible for them to eliminate much of their guesswork a to what services they must provide ahead for, said John Nolen in *City Planning (2nd ed.). New York; Appleton, 1929,* shortly after zoning was enacted in New York. Hubbard and Hubbard wrote: "The utility companies as a rule may be counted favorable to zoning. The general attitude of the telephone companies has been expressed in favor of the stability brought about by zoning." H. V. Hubbard and T.K. Hubbard, *Our Cities Today and Tomorrow.* Cambridge: Harvard University Press, 1929, p. 176.

22 Hubbard and Hubbard. *Our Cities Today and Tomorrow,* op. cit., p. 282.

23 Arthur B. Smith and William L. Campbell. *Automatic Telephony,* New York: McGraw–Hill, 1915, p. 379.

24 In the early years there was considerable concern about telephone wires and safety. The *American Architect and Building News* had a section in each issue on new inventions. It did not note the telephone in 1876, but by 1881 there had been ten references to the telephone in the magazine; four of these concerned safety. There was particular concern about the proliferation of overhead wires (Cf. section 6.2.).

25 Charles Malford Robinson. *Improvement of Towns and Cities,* New York: G. P. Putnam and Sons, 1901.

26 Ebenezer Howard. *Garden Cities of Tomorrow.* Louden: Faber and Faber, 1945.

27 Hubbard and Hubbard. *Our Cities Today and Tomorrow,* p. 93.

28 Cf. President's Research Committee on Social Trends, *Recent Social Trends in the United States.* New York: McGraw-Hill, 1933, pp. 197ff.

29 Hubbard and Hubbard. *Our Cities Today and Tomorrow,* p. 185.

30 Arthur Pound. *The Telephone Idea: Fifty Years After.* New York: Greenberg, 1926.

[31] Theodore K. Noss. *Resistance to Social Innovations*. Chicago: University of Chicago, Dept. of Sociology, 1944.

[32] In Ithiel de Sola Pool, et al, *The Telephone's First Century–and Beyond*, Thomas Y. Crowell Company, New York, 1977, p. 11.

[33] E.g. Rural Telephones. *Telephony*, Oct. 1901, 2 (4); Farmer's Telephones, *Telephony*, April, 1902, 3 (4), 117; The Rural Telephone. Sept. 1902, 4 (3), 144–5; Rural Telephones. July, 1904, 10 (1), 34; The Telephone in the Country. *Telephony*, July, 1905, 10 (1), 52; The Farm Telephone. *Telephony*, Jan. 1908, 16 (1), 23; Value of Rural Telephones. *Telephony*, Aug., 1906, 12 (2), 117. See also Telephones in Rural Districts. *Board of Agriculture Journal,* July 1911, 18 326–8; Wilbur Wheeler Bassett. Telephones in the Country. Reprinted in Ray Brousseau, *Looking Forward.* New York: American Heritage, 1970.

[34] The Teeming Country, from Point of View. *Scribner's Magazine,* April, 1912, 51, 506–7.

[35] Hendrick. Telephones for the Millions, *McClures Magazine,* Oct. 1914, 44, 51–52. Cf. Rural Telephones Down South, *Telephony,* April 1908, 15 (4) 269.

[36] Cf. section 5.2.4.

[37] The Telephone in Government Service, *Telephony,* June 1905, 9 (6), 507.

[38] Weather Forecasts to Farmers by Telephone, *Telephony*. July 1904, 8. (1) 32: Hendrick. Telephones for the Millions. p. 53.

[39] Hendrick. *op. cit.*

[40] Rural Electrification Administration. *Rural Telephone Service.* Washington, D. C.: U.S. Government Printing Office, 1960, p. 3.

[41] W. W. Bassett. Telephones in the Country. Reprinted without citation of source in Ray Brousseau. *Looking forward* (a compendium of articles from the turn of the century). New York: American Heritage Press. 1970, p. 81. See also The Telephone in Rural Districts. *Board of Agriculture Journal,* no author (England). 1911 18, 326-8.

[42] Bassett. Telephones in the Country, p.81

[43] Hendricks. Telephones for the Millions, pp 52-53.

[44] Value of Rural Telephones, *Telephony,* Aug. 1906, 117. This point is repeated with reference to Canada in 12 (2), *Telephony,* Mar. 1907, 13 (3), 183.

[45] Telephones Help the Farmer, *Telephony,* April 1908, 15 (4), 243.

[46] The Teeming Country, pp. 506-7.

[47] Rural Electrification Administration, *Rural Telephone Service;* News Service By Telephone, *Telephony,* Nov. 1906, 12 (5), 297.

[48] Cf. Back to the Land— and the Telephone, *The Spectator,* (London), April 7, 1906., pp. 530-31. Rider Haggard proposed a new remedy for rural depopulation by putting "a telephone in every cottage."

[49] Spread of the Rural Telephone Movement, *Scientific American,* 1911, 104, 162.

[50] Hendricks. Telephones for the Millions, p. 51.

[51] The peak year for the number of mutual telephone systems was 1927. (Rural Electrification Administration, *Rural Telephone Service.*)

[52] REA. *Rural Telephone Services.*

[53] *U.S. Department of Agriculture, Crop Reporting Board, Statistical Reporting Service, Number of Farms 1910-1959—Land and Farms 1950-1959 By States.* Washington D.C.: U.S. Government Printing Office, June 1962, no. 316.

[54] Casson. The Social Value of the Telephone p. 905.

[55] REA. *Rural Telephone Service;* Vail, Public Utilities and Public Policies. *Atlantic Monthly,* Vol. 3, pp. 315-319, March 1913.In February 1910 an article on The Telephone and the Investor in *American Review of Reviews, 41,* 246 compared a cooperative exchange in Grand Rapids with a Bell exchange. The former charged $.25 a month to residential subscribers; the latter $3.00. Such low rates by rural independents were possible because they typically had under 100 subscribers on a system.

[56] For description of such systems see Cheap Telephone System for Farmers, *Scientific American,* 1900, 2 (4) *82,* 196; Rural Telephones, *Telephony,* Oct. 1901 pp. 150-151; Farmers' Telephones, *Telephony,* Apr. 1902, *3* (4), 117; The Rural Telephone, *Telephony,* Sept. 1902, *4* (3) 77 144-51; Telephones in Rural Districts, *Board of Agriculture Journal (England), 1911, 18,* 326-8.

[57] The rapid growth of independents did force a change of policy on the Bell System. The original policy of the System had been only to lease phones, not to sell them; to lease them only to companies which joined the system; and to restrict the growth of other companies by declining to interconnect with them. After the expiration of the Bell patents, however, phones became available from rival sources to independent phone companies. In 1907, therefore, Vail reversed the policy and allowed Western Electric phones to be sold to other companies; indeed, by gradually lifting the ban on interconnection, he encouraged independents to develop relatively unprofitable rural areas. For the Vail 1907 memo, see Walker Report, vol. 1, Report on Engineering and Research Departments of the Bell System, 1937, Appendix I; Federal Communications Commission, *Investigation of the Telephone Industry in the United States.*

[58] The percent of telephones in the U.S. not connected with the Bell System decreased from 37% *in 1900 to 8% in 1918:*

[59] Brousseau. Looking Forward, *Header.* p. 81

3

The Phone and the Economy

3.1 Industrial organization.

3.1.1 The telephone will foster management from a distance. (Type A)

We pick up here from the point made above (2.1.1) that the phone fostered the separation of plant and office. In general it made it feasible to conduct operations that were scattered over dispersed geographic locations. The *Scientific American* made that point about the phone in 1914 in an article called "Action at a Distance."

> A man in charge of many business interests might sit in his study and communicate accurately, rapidly and effectively with them all far more successfully than he could by passing from one office to another, attending one board meeting, another committee meeting and generally endeavoring to convey his own body where he really needs to convey only his own ideas.[1]

The telephone permitted the growth in the size of industrial organizations, and permitted businessmen to control these vast complexes from a distance. Morgan's partner George W. Perkins used a system he called "rapid transit telephony" to call ten to thirty bankers in a row to raise capital.[2] Harriman also used the phone continuously in that way, as we shall see below (3.2.1)

3.1.2 The telephone will favor the growth of large firms. (2) (Type B)

For one thing, the telephone company itself rapidly became a corporate giant. By 1912 telephony was the fourth largest industry in the United States. Not only was AT&T large (as were also its sister organizations in other countries); it was well managed, and one of the fountainheads of modern theories of scientific management.

More important, the existence of a telephone network facilitated the creation of great industrial complexes having activities in many locations.

59

Indeed that is a better way of describing the process than trying to fit it to the simple categories of centralization or decentralization. Bringing dispersed activity under one management was centralization, but permitting an organization's activities to be geographically separated is decentralization.

Indeed this dual process of concentration and dispersion of power was observed at the time. Casson commented in 1910 that "the telephone arrived in time to prevent big corporations from becoming unwieldly and aristocratic."

By 1937 a classic economic analysis of the relation of communication to centralization and decentralization was published. Ronald Coase's paper "The Nature of the Firm"[3] concluded that communication improvements may either increase or decrease the optimum size of firm, depending upon whether interfirm or intrafirm costs drop more as a result.

3.1.3 Use of the long distance telephone will reduce the authority of field office managers. (Type B)

It was often asserted that the introduction of the long distance phone (and also the telegraph earlier) resulted in field managers being lowered from plenipotentiary agents to errand boys. That point has been made about branch bank managers who used to be partners making decisions for themselves, and now are described as just employees,[4] about ambassadors, and about managers of industrial and commercial field locations. It was also made in an article in *Telephony* in 1906 regarding political field managers: "It has curtailed the functions and responsibilities of a district manager as the cable has those of an ambassador."[5] The point was made regarding all large organizations.

The reduction of the power of field managers is most often perceived as a centralization of power. Westrum, for example, points out that before the telephone, business, government and military instructions to field agents tended to be vague because the chief could not anticipate the circumstances in which they would be carried out.[6] Page in 1932[7] described letters of instructions to ship captains that the Business Historical Society had compiled. "They are nearly all vague and indefinite, because the merchant had no idea of what the prevailing price of his goods would be when they reached Canton, Tobago, and Manila."[8] But the new ability of the "boss" at the center to interfere directly in details in the field does not necessarily mean a concentration of power, even if it means a decline in the power of the field agent. Marshall McLuhan describes the same process as decentralization.[9]

> One of the most startling consequences of the telephone was its intro-
> duction of a "seamless web" of interlaced patterns in management and
> decision-making. It is not feasible to exercise delegated authority by tele-

phone. The pyramidal structure . . . cannot withstand the speed of the phone to bypass all hierarchical arrangements. . . . Today the junior executive can get on a first-name basis with seniors in different parts of the country.[10]

3.1.4 The telephone will democratize hierarchic relations. (Type B)

We may continue the McLuhan quote from above.

> If delegated chain-of-command authority won't work by telephone but only by written instruction, what sort of authority does come into play? . . . On the telephone only the authority of knowledge will work.[11]

Both Boettinger[12] and Cherry[13] present the case that the telephone was a democratizing instrument and quote various expressions of concern about that. That general process of democratization in society is something we shall take up in Section 4.8. The special aspect of interest here is the tendency in large organizations for people making phone calls to skip over normal channels of hierarchy to a greater extent than they do in written communications or in appointments. The literature of the period we are studying repeatedly asserts that that happens, as in Casson's statement already quoted about the president of the steel trust talking to a formen in a mine.

3.2 Capital markets.

The impact of the telephone system on finance was at least as great as that on industry. And as in the case of industrial organization the effects came two ways: through the creation of a new giant enterprise, the phone company, and through the use of the phone system by financiers.

3.2.1 The creation of a telephone system will require large scale financing. (Type C)

The telephone industry rapidly became one of the most important fund raisers in the money markets.[14] It secured its first million in capital in 1879. By 1910 it was worth more than 3/4 of a billion dollars; by 1913, $924 million.[15] In 1912, total investment in all companies in the iron and steel industry was $16 per capita, in lumber and timber $13, in illuminating and heating gas $10, and in telephony, fourth, $9 per capita.[16] In that same year the capital cost of the British system was £25,000,000 or $100,000,000.[17]

Ultimately, one of the important features of the telephone industry was the dominance of AT&T, a single company. Thus unlike other new industries (electric power for example) which consisted of many separate companies, telephony introduced a new and unique element of size into the money markets. Next to government bonds, telephone securities have become a foundation of institutional portfolios. Whatever happens to the prospects of AT&T has ripple effects on financial institutions comparable to those of what happens to the prospects of tax exempt municipals.

AT&T did not always have that primate position. During the two decades when the independents blossomed (1894 until World War I) a major part of the secret of their temporary success was diverse access to funding. The primary limit on the Bell System's growth in 1907, when Vail for the second time, took over as President was capital. By a natural process, given the importance of raising capital, control of the Bell System passed in 1881 from the original innovators, first to financiers under the presidency of Forbes[18] and then in 1907 to the house of Morgan in New York, one of the few organizations in a position to raise the necessary funds.

The ultimate decline and assimilation of the independents was attributable primarily to the technical disadvantage for their subscribers of not being interconnected with the national network. Their financial weakness compared to the Bell System was an important mechanism in the process. As already noted, they tried to undercut the Bell System's prices, and therefore often failed to amortize their investments. When, as a result of technical progress or just of growth, the time came for refinancing, they were often in trouble and frequently had to turn to AT&T for capital and affiliation.

Vail and his co-organizers of AT&T recognized from the start the dependence of their system's growth on capital and, consequently, on sound financing practices. We have no evidence that they aniticpated that the company that they were starting, by its very size, would come to be a major foundation of the nation's pension trusts, universities, and financial institutions.

In other countries one of the main reasons why phone systems have been nationalized is that their managements have not been strong enough to command the capital they needed from the private money market, or the nation's financial system was not developed enough to provide the needed capital domestically. The options of having an undercapitalized, poorly-working phone system, or an internationally capitalized and, therefore, foreign controlled one, both seemed less attractive than a phone system capitalized under the credit of the national treasury.

Thus, one effect of the building of national phone systems has been to create a large demand for capital, and this has strengthened the institutions that could, depending on circumstances, provide the needed capital—the banking system, foreign investors, or the state bureaucracy, as the case might be.

3.2.2 The phone system will facilitate the conduct of financial transactions. (Type A)

Among all spheres of business, three are most dependent upon communications: transport, the press, and finance. Today these run up the largest bills for communications services, and even before Bell's day, these were the main users of the telegraph and the main leasors of private telegraph lines.

Three reasons why financial institutions are so dependent upon communication facilities are that 1) for them "time means money," 2) the "goods" they deal in are documents, and 3) financiers are businessmen's businessmen. Their activities are outwardly oriented. Their in-house processing activities are relatively trivial; their important activities involve contact with a wide variety of external organizations.

3.2.2.1 The telephone will speed the conduct of finance. (Type A)

In banking, time literally means money. To save one day in the processing of a transfer of $1 million, saves $137.00, assuming only a 5 percent interest rate. Clearly one will process such a transfer by cable or by phone rather than posting a letter.

Bankers and brokers were already using the telegraph for routine transactions when the phone came along. They quickly recognized the extra value of the telephone for those transactions requiring discussion and persuasion. Herbert Casson reported that George W. Perkins of J.P. Morgan, " 'is the only man . . . who can raise twenty millions in twenty minutes.' "[19] According to Burton J. Hendrick, Edward H. Harriman, "once dramatically saved the Erie Railroad from bankruptcy by timely use of a bedside telephone."[20]

3.2.2.2 The telephone will reduce speculative fluctuations. (Type B)

In the theory of a perfect market it is assumed that the buyer and seller have full knowledge, i.e., each buyer and seller should know what is being bid and asked. Where information is imperfect trades may take place in different parts of the market at different prices, and speculation may be profitable.

Rapid telephonic communication served to improve the market and reduce speculation. In Section 2.2.1.5 we noted some examples in agriculture: farmers were enabled to learn the price of their crop in town, and not be dependent on the representations of a travelling agent. Bankers used the telephone in similar ways on a national scale. Casson describes how they used the phone to lessen the impact of the panic of 1907.

At the height of the storm, on a Saturday evening, the New York
bankers met in an almost desperate conference. They decided, as an emergency measure of self-protection, not to ship cash to Western banks. At
midnight they telephoned this decision to the bankers of Chicago and St.
Louis. These men, in turn, conferred by telephone, and on Sunday after-
noon called up the bankers of neighboring states. And so the news went
from "phone to phone," until by Monday morning all bankers and chief
depositors were aware of the situation, and prepared for the team play that
prevented any general disaster.[21]

3.3 The labor market.

The telephone also had various effects on labor. It created new jobs,
destroyed others, and affected methods of hiring.

3.3.1 The telephone system will open up new job opportunities. (Type B)

Particularly important among the employment opportunities offered by the
telphone system were jobs as operators for women. We discuss that topic in Section
9.4.2. Also important were the employment opportunities for technically trained
persons, discussed under the heading of education in Section 11.1.1. In addition the
phone system offered a reasonably secure and progressive career opportunity to
large numbers of employees.

3.3.2 The phone system pioneers in scientific management and labor relations. (Type C)

Because the phone system is such a large employer it must necessarily have a
sophisticated hiring, training, and labor management system. The phone
company, however, was not the only large employer. Sheer numbers do not
distinguish it from the Post Office, Department of Defense, or a few other major
institutions. As important as its size was the rapidity of its growth and the
uniqueness of its job requirements. Thousands of operators. linesmen, and
installers had to be trained every year. Operator turnover was about 30% per
annum.[22]

AT&T developed carefully designed and scientifically based techniques of
training and personnel management. They also built up a folklore and mythos
about the heroism and service of operators and linesmen, reporting outstanding
performances in their magazine ads.[23]

3.3.3 Messenger jobs will decline with the development of the telephone. (Type B)

Today we have forgotten how numerous and important messenger boys
once were. They were as central in every office as typists are today. They were part

of the passing scene on the streets. The only way to communicate with a person at a distance was to have someone carry the message. Part way it might go by telegraph, but even then the last leg was by messenger boy.

The telephone was immediately recognized to be a threat to messenger boys. A telephone advocate put the accent on the positive and said in 1911 that the spread of the telephone would allow the Western Union messenger boys to stay in school.[24] That was one view of child labor, but others stressed unemployment and loss of earning power.

3.3.4 The development of the telephone is affected by the availability of messenger boys. (Type A)

If the telephone and messenger boys competed, then the converse to the problem of phone competition to messenger boys was to recognize that messenger boys were competition to the phone. In 1879, Sir William Preece, the Chief Engineer of the British Post Office, testified to a special committee of the House of Commons that the telephone had little future in Britain. "There are conditions in America which necessitate the use of such instruments more than here. Here we have a superabundance of messengers. . . . The absence of servants has compelled Americans to adopt communication systems."[25]

3.3.5 Jobs for telegraphers decline with the development of the telephone. (Type B)

The other major occupational group whose jobs were seriously impacted by the telephone were Morse code telegraphers. We shall discuss their situation below. (7.2.2)

3.3.6 Jobs for operators are reduced by automatic dialing. (Type A)

As we have already noted in Section 1.2.1, the introduction of automatic dialing in the U.S. was motivated by the impossible prospective requirement for operators under a growing manual system. The displacement of operators was not sudden, for the telephone monopoly introduced automatic switching equipment gradually. Also, the transition was eased by the large turnover among operators, many of whom were working prior to marriage; and the total system was growing. So the shift was not a crisis, but it was a major transition.

3.3.7 The telephone will increase job mobility. (Type B)

The telephone made it easier for employers and employees to contact each other. Want ads list telephone numbers. Employment agencies phone unemployed workers when an appropriate job comes along.

That, of course, presumes that the poor have telephones, and so such practices have become common only in the last couple of decades, since phones in the U.S. have become almost universal. Indeed, the role of the telephone as a job finding device has led social agencies to conclude that the telephone is a necessity, not a luxury, and that the phone bill is a legitimate charge on welfare budgets.

3.3.8 The telephone will reduce the use of hiring halls. (Type B)

Where employment comes and goes day by day, as for longshoremen, some device is needed for swift contact with the labor force. The hiring hall was one such device, and one that strengthened the power of the union, for daily it had workers sitting around together in a group. But rather than idle their day away at the hiring hall, workers would prefer to stay at home and to be phoned. This is increasingly the practice, to the detriment of unions.

3.4 Merchandising.

3.4.1 The telephone will be used for shopping. (Type A)

Today, when there is a great deal of blue sky talk about the replacement of stores by on-line terminal-shopping from the home, it is enlightening to look at actual experience of telephone shopping. There is a great deal of it. Some few housewives do almost all their shopping by phone. Most buyers occasionally order some things over the phone. And let us not forget the wholesale field: in large areas practically all ordering is done by phone; the retailer often has an established relationship with a series of wholesalers, and once a day or once a week he phones in what he needs in order to replenish his supply.

Yet, as important as telephone buying has become, it has by no means displaced the shop. That is not because telephone marketing is immature; it is one of the oldest uses of the telephone. The prospect of the housewife placing her order by telephone was there from the beginning. H. G. Wells in 1902 discussed telephone shopping, but correctly forecast that much shopping would still be done in person: "it will still be natural for shops to be gathered together in some central place."[26]

Around 1905, department stores began to turn to the telephone. Prior to June 1, 1905, only one department store in the U.S. had telephone ordering facilities. Several installed them shortly thereafter,[27] placing phones on each counter.[28] By November 1906, *Telephony* reported that one store had 2,000 telephones in use and received 70,000 messages a day.[29] Some New York stores, as early as 1905, experimented with taking telephone orders at night.[30]

Also noted frequently was the usefulness to farmers of the combination of the phone, parcel post, and RFD for mail order shopping.[31] There were also some more novel but less successful ideas for telephone marketing. A Connecticut grocery store installed free telephones in the homes of customers to encourage them to order.[32] A Congressman suggested the institution of special low farm-to-kitchen telephone rates, to enable consumers to order direct from the grower without intervention of middlemen.[33]

Indeed, one has the impression that telephone retailing has not developed to the extent that early enthusiasts expected. It has, to some degree, become a luxury service since it does not economize on labor; it requires a salesclerk to converse with the customer, one on one. The economics of mass merchandising have moved in the direction of self-service. Indeed some kinds of telephone shopping were more common in the days before supermarkets, when housewive had a personal relation with a grocer, butcher, and ice man. That trend away from personalized shopping was not anticipated by the early writers on the telephone. Interactive terminals are responsive to the new trend toward reducing labor costs, and so may have a promising future.

3.4.2 The telephone will speed movement of perishable goods. (Type A)

One of the merchandising areas where telephone use was adopted most quickly was in the ordering and distribution of perishable goods. A 1906 article on "The Sociological Effects of the Telephone" describes how oyster barge men were put out of business because retauranteurs could phone their orders directly to the oysters planters.[34]

3.4.3 The telephone will broaden market areas. (Type A)

Particularly with the aid of the yellow pages, the telephone has made it easier to do comparison shopping or to hunt around for exactly the service that one wants. In that way it not only eliminates middlemen or jobbers,[35] but also allows search over a larger area. That became increasingly so with the gradual fall in long distance rates, with direct distance dialing, and with the introduction of "800" numbers.[36]

3.4.4. The telephone will reduce the travels of salesmen. (Type A)

Travelling salesmen continued to call on customers after the phone, but they found that they had to come in person less often, could phone between visits, and for some purposes could prepare for a visit by a phone call.[37]

3.4.5 The telephone will be used for advertising canvassing. (Type A)

We reserve a fuller treatment of this topic for discussion in Section 4.6, where we deal with the use of the telephone for polling, canvassing, and similar activities. We note it here also because one of the major uses of such canvassing is to sell prodcuts. We shall note that some cultures tolerate such unsolicited calls and others do not.

3.5 The telephone increases productivity. (Type B)

This statement could perhaps be construed as simply a summary of everything we have said in this section on the telephone and the economy, or more accurately it is a statement about a consequence of all those developments. The phone increases productivity by reducing speculative fluctuations, speeding financial transactions, increasing labor mobility, making easier the management of geographically dispersed units, etc. The telephone also increases productivity in a myriad of ways we have not separately listed. It permits coordination of pieces of that complex clockwork which is the economic system. It is used millions of times a day to control production, shipping, recording, and selling. It permits the operation of a complex division of labor. All of that was recognized from early on.

"Suppose that at midday to-morrow, just when the great engine of American business is surging away at top tension, every wire of those millions of miles should without an instant's warning die," asked John Kimberly Mumford in 1908.[38]

FOOTNOTES

[1] Action at a Distance, p. 39.

[2] Aronson. Bell's Electric toy p. 28.

[3] Ronald Coase, The Nature of the Firm, *Economica*, Nov. 1937 *4*, 389405.

[4] Fritz Redlich (1952) quoted in Ronald M. Westrum. The Historical Impact of Communication Technology on Organization. (Institute for the Study of Social Change, Working Paper no. 56) unpublished manuscript, Purdue University, 1976.

[5] Telephone in Politics, *Telephony*, Dec. 1906 *12* (6), 364.

[6] Westrum. *Historical Impact, of Communication Technology on Organization*, p. 7.

[7] Arthur W. Page. Social Aspects of Communication Development, in Page (Ed.), *Modern Communication. Boston: Houghton Mifflin, 1932.*

[8] Page describes episodes in which the Rothschilds after the battle of Waterloo, and speculators in the early years of the U.S. government, made killings by having rapid couriers bring information that others did not have.

[9] Marshall McLuhan. *Understanding Media;* New York.; New American Library, 1964, p. 234.

[10] McLuhan. *Understanding Media*, p. 238.

[11] McLuhan. *Understanding Media*, p. 238.

[12] Henry M. Boettinger, Our Sixth-and-a-half Sense, In Pool, *The Social Impact of the Telephone.*

[13] Cherry. The Telephone System.

[14] Cf. J. Warren Stehman. *The Financial History of the American Telephone and Telegraph Company*. Boston: Houghton Mifflin, 1925.

[15] Albert W. Atwood. Finance, *Harper's Weekly*, 1913, *58*, p. 29–31.

[16] Henry Smith Williams. The Growth of the Telephone. *Science*, 1912, *22*, 105–6.

[17] The Government Telephone in England. *The Literary Digest*,1912, *44*, 153–4.

[18] Forbes became President in 1879 two years before control passed from the Bell family.

[19] J.P. Morgan quoted in Casson. The Social Value of the Telephone, p. 900.

[20] Hendrick. Telephones for the Millions, p. 50.

[21] Casson. The Social Value of the Telephone, p. 901.

[22] Good Points and Bad Points of Telephone Operating as a Trade for Philadelphia Girls *The Survey* Feb. 17, 1914, *31*, 543.

[23] E.g., Lineman's Devotion to His Job, *Literary Digest*, Vol. 48, part 1 1914, pp. 572, 573, 575, 576: Enos A. Mills, Linemen Heroes at the Crest of the Continent *Colliers*, April 19, 1913, *51*, p. 14.

[24] Casson. The Future of the Telephone, pp. 12903–12918.

[25] Cf. Pool et al. Forsight and Hindsight: The Case of the Telephone, In Pool, *The Social Impact of the Telephone*, p. 128; Dilts, p. 11.

[26] Wells. *Anticipations*, p. 61.

[27] The Department Store and the Telephone *Telephony*, Dec. 19, 1908, *16* (19), 639–40.

[28] Ralph Bergengren. The Far-Flung Telephone *World Today*, Dec. 1905, *10*, 69.

[29] The Indispensable Telephone, *Telephony*, Nov. 1906, *12* (15), 296.

[30] Shopping at Night by Telephone, *Telephony*, Sept. 1905, 10 *(3)*, 221.

[31] Cf. Hendricks, Telephones for the Millions, p. 52.

[32] Free Business Telephone, *Telephony*, July 1907, *14* (1), 37.

[33] Lewis. Congressional Record, March 4, 1915, op. cit., p. 847.

[34] The Sociological Effects of the Telephone, *Scientific American*, 1906, *94*, 500.

[35] The Sociological Effects of the Telephone. *Scientific American,* 1906, *94*,500.: also *Telephony*, 6, Dec. 1906, *12*, (6), 353.

[36] 800 numbers are for inbound WATS Lines, where the vendor provides free long distance calling to the customer.

[37] Cf. The Telephone in Modern Business, *Telephony*, Nov. 1901, *2*, (5), 190–91; that article claimed that there was a visible effect on railroad traffic.

[38] Mumford. This land of Opportunity, Application of the Modern Telephone, *Telephony*, Aug, 1902, *4* (2), 94–95, which attributes the U.S. lead in productivity to the telephone.

4

The Phone and the Polity

The effects of the telephone on political organizations in some respects parallel its effects on economic organizations; both belong to the genus large organizations. But some phone effects are specific to politics.

4.1 The telephone system will foster national integration. (Type B)

As long distance telephony spread its reach over the nation, observers proclaimed that it meant "a final blow to sectionalism. . . . Had the telephone system reached its present perfection previous to 1861," Arthur Pound argued in the semi-centennial volume on the phone system, "the Civil War would not have occurred."[1] More commonly, writers have made similar statements about broadcasting which is said to have homogenized the popular culture, but the telephone too was seen as reducing sectionalism even before national broadcasting had become a major phenomenon.

4.1.1 The long distance telephone will reduce regional dialect differences. (Type B)

The most commonly cited indicator of national integration is the disappearance of sectional dialects.[2]

Edward J. Hall, president of the Southern Bell Telephone and Telegraph Company is quoted in two articles in *Telephony*. Each article says virtually the same thing: there are to be no more dialects—no southern, no northern, no western accent—but instead just "one harmonious American language"

> spoken in exactly the same intonation throughout the length and breadth of the land . . . The Southern accent, too, is rapidly disappearing. There are many causes—the southerner travels more, he uses the language of commerce to-day . . . but, above all, looms the fact that long distance telephone is used so much more generally and frequently. The use of the

71

telephone, little as the casual onlooker may think of it, is bringing all normal voices to a sameness of pitch and engrafting a simplicity in enunciation."[3]

To anyone who has followed the recent literature on radio and television as the alleged causes of the disappearance of regional accents and of the emergence of a standard national language, it is astonishing to find this same set of statements in 1906, and ascribed to the telephone. Given the tiny numbers of people who were making interregional telephone calls in 1906 (compared to the enormous number who were listening to radio 20 years later), it is hard to be persuaded of Mr. Hall's causal attribution, yet the trend was taking place. The pace of interregional traffic and intercourse of all sorts had begun to pick up, and with it a process of national homogenization to which the telephone and later the radio each contributed.

4.2 A telephone system will foster growth in the scale of government administration. (Type B)

Just as the telephone fosters the growth of big business, so it also permits big government to function.

The first phones in Washington were set up when Congress appropriated $150 in 1878 to connect the Public Printer's office with the Capitol, to enable members of Congress to order extra copies of their speeches.[4] A phone installed in the White House in the same year (during Rutherford B. Hayes' administration) went largely unused.[5]

The telephone came into significant government use during the first two decades of this century. Writing in 1911, Herbert Casson notes,

> Public officials, even in the United States, have been slow to change from the old-fashioned and more dignified use of written documents and uniformed messengers; but in the last ten years there has been a sweeping revolution in this respect . . . the new idea [use of the telephone] has already arrived in the more efficient departments of the Federal service.[6]

Presidents differed in their attitudes to the telephone. Presidents Cleveland and Harrison did not use the device much and only one instrument existed in the White House. President Garfield possessed a demonstration model while still a Congressman in 1878. William McKinley was the first who used the telephone extensively. He ran his 1896 Presidential campaign by telephone from Canton, Ohio, including listening to the proceedings of the Republican Convention in Chicago. A small switchboard was installed in the White House in 1901.

By 1910, Waldon Fawcett was able to report, in an article in *Telephony*, that "every Federal official, from the President to the humblest subordinate of the nation's public servants, has a telephone on his desk." The phone systems at the capitol and the War Department and that of the Navy were ranked among the world's largest private exchanges, in number of phones and number of calls handled daily. By means of the vast telephone networks set up in the nation's capital, the President could communicate with the Secretaries of State, War, Navy, Interior, Agriculture, Treasury, Commerce, and Labor, with the Attorney General and the Postmaster General at their offices; in addition, he could reach, by means of direct tie lines to the Capitol, the President of the Senate or the Speaker of the House.[7] However, in the following election the president chosen was Woodrow Wilson who, as we shall see later, disliked the phone and declined to use it. (cf. 4.5.2.) By 1931, when the new Department of Commerce Building was opened, it contained 1600 telephones carrying 10,000 calls a day.[8]

Franklin D. Roosevelt was probably the last president who did not make much use of the phone. In 1934, according to the log books at Hyde Park, about 200 persons a day called his phone, but he only actually talked on the phone about five times a day. If one visits the "Little White House" in Georgia, where he spent much of his last years and from which he ran the war effort, one will find only one phone and that in a basement room. Roosevelt preferred personal contact and written correspondence to telephoning. He built his political machine and national status by an enormous correspondence carried out by means of a team of writers under the leadership of Stephen Early. When he reached the White House this team was expanded to handle the vast flow of letters that he invited in his radio fireside chats.[9] Roosevelt, however, was probably the last President to view the telephone with distaste. All his successors have been heavy users, and particularly Jack Kennedy and Jimmy Carter have been telecommunications enthusiasts.

As in the case of industrial organizations, the diametrically opposite consequences of centralization and decentralization, gigantism and democratization have been attributed to the growth in governmental telephony. And as in the case of industry both sets of assertions have some merit. The organization grew larger with the aid of the telephone, yet the duality of effects is illustrated by the fact that by allowing flexibility and informality the telephone prevented the bureaucratic giant from strangling itself.

4.2.1 The use of the telphone will centralize the exercise of authority. (Type B)

In section 3.1.3 we noted the proposition that long distance telephony (along with telegraphy) tended to reduce the authority of field office managers. Among examples that have been cited are the decline in the authority of ambassadors. A similar effect has been observed even within local or headquarters administration. The telephone permits the top official to intervene quickly and directly in any office of the organization and thus keep close personal touch.[10]

4.2.2 The use of the telephone will reduce the bureaucratic rigidity of administrative behavior. (Type B)

We can repeat the point made in the last paragraph to draw an apparently opposite conclusion. A chief executive who picks up the phone to talk informally to a subordinate several levels down the bureaucratic tree, or two subordinate officials from different branches of an organization talking informally to one another without informing their chiefs, are breaking the structure of bureaucratic authority. They are avoiding passing messages through the line of command. As Casson pointed out in the quotation above, they have changed from "the old-fashioned and more dignified use of written documents" which could be physically passed from hand to hand along the line of command. We note later an 1899 Supreme Court description of long distance government communication as "almost all, if not all, in writing." (Section 4.3.1) However, the kind of bureaucratic formalism of communication that the Supreme Court noted broke down under the impact of the telephone's convenience for direct person-to-person access.

4.2.3 The use of the telphone will reduce the keeping of written records. (Type B)[11]

Given the vast proliferation of government files it is hard to believe that more could be in writing than is. But it could be. Everyone with experience in government can testify that many of the most important understandings are reached on the telephone, precisely to avoid the creation of a written file. Consequences of this for historians we shall note in section 11.3.2.

4.3 Legal effects of the telephone.

The courts had to take early note of telephones and of some novel problems they raised. Phone companies, like any large companies, were in the courts in many ordinary ways that we do not take account of here. These included patent suits, liability for damage from accidents, workman's compensation, and contracts. We deal with the subject of regulation in a separate section (4.4.2). Here we note a number of novel legal issues that the telephone raised and how the courts handled them.

4.3.1 Courts subsume the telephone under established legal precedents, particularly those of telegraphy. (Type C)

The issue of whether the telephone was a telegraph under the law, and therefore governed by regulations over telegraphy, was resolved in the affirmative in Britain in 1880.[12] It was discussed in American Law journals promptly thereafter.[13] In 1887 the first of a series of similar decisions appeared in the U.S. courts.[14] However, in one very important case the Supreme Court refused to follow that analogy. In Richmond v. Southern Bell Telephone and Telegraph Co. (174 US 761, 1899) the Court held that the provisions of the 1866 Post Roads Act allowing telegraph companies use of lumber and free right of way on public lands and along post roads did not apply to the telephone. The judge argued that in 1866 "nothing was then distinctly known of any device by which articulate speech could be electrically transmitted or received between different points more or less distant from each other."[15]

The court then made the point that "Governmental communications to all distant points are almost all, if not all, in writing. The useful Government privileges which formed an important element in the legislation would be entirely inapplicable to telephone lines, by which oral communications only are transmitted. . . ."[16]

That decision deprived phone companies of some useful privileges, though the reverse British decision did them more harm in the British context by extending *de jure* the public monopoly status of the telegraph to the telephone; private telephone companies were allowed by the British Government to maintain a precarious existence until 1912, but they existed only on sufferance.

Despite the Richmond case, the general impulse of U.S. courts was to pretend that the phone was nothing new. Precedents from telegraphy and also from common carrier law were taken over into the telphone field.

4.3.2 The telephone raises problems in the law of evidence. (Type C)

Very early the question arose as to the admissability in court of John Doe's statement that Richard Roe had made some agreement with him during a telephone conversation.[17] There was no doubt that oral agreements had standing in the law, but could Doe, when he only heard a telephonic voice and could not see Roe, be sure it was Roe who was talking to him. In 1885 the Supreme Court of Kentucky in Sullivan v. Kuykendall decided that acceptance of such testimony would be subversive of recognized rules of evidence.[18] Other courts, however, soon recognized that:

> The telephone although a very recent invention, has come into such common use that, we think . . . that the courts may properly take judicial notice of the general manner and extent to which it is made use of by the business community. No doubt very many important business transactions are every day made by telephonic communications of precisely the same character as that which the witness was allowed to testify in this case.[19]

The debate continued for a couple of decades[20] but ultimately the courts had to adapt to the realities of the vast increase of telephone use in business, and perhaps were also reassured by improved fidelity in telephone reception.

4.3.3 The use of the telephone raises problems as to the liability of the phone company for losses attendant on telephone failures. (Type C)

Perhaps discussion of this proposition does not belong here, for the basic principle had already been established in telegraph law that the carrier if not grossly negligent was liable only for the value of the undelivered physical message, not for the value of the information contained in it. In contrast to transportation common carriers who could be held liable for the value of the lost or damaged cargo, the message carrier moved something that had no obvious intrinsic value that the carrier could recognize. The carrier could not be expected to assume a potentially unlimited liability for whatever value some information might have to its users in unknown circumstances.

While there was that telegraphic precedent, the telephone entered into American life in such a full way that numerous cases were nonetheless brought, making such claims. A child died without benefit of a physician when the phone failed to work; businesses lost money when their customers could not reach them or when they were mislisted in the phone book. Between 1881 and 1902 courts of 25 states made rulings that removed telephone companies from possible suits under the mental anguish doctrine. The cases on liability were reviewed by Brutus Clay in 1914; he presents arguments, similar to those in the telegraph case cited above.[21] For those reasons the courts generally declined to hold phone companies liable for all the consequences of a failure of service.

4.3.4 Telephonic communication suffers a diminished First Amendment protection compared to earlier means of communication. (Type C)

The traditional domain to which the principles of the First Amendment have been applied are face-to-face meetings and private publishing. Electrical communication systems that require the stringing of wires across public and private lands and that are conducted by local monopolies have not been treated by the courts as subject to the same exemption from government regulation. For example, the Supreme Court has thrown out special taxes on newspapers as unconstitutional; it allows taxes on telephone bills.

Denial of the telephone to a subscriber for having used bad language goes back to 1885. Denial of a printing press to a publisher because of the obscenity of previous publications would be unconstitutional prior restraint under the doctrine of Near v. Minnesota.[22]

Pugh v. City and Suburban Tel. Co., 9 Bull 104, held that "if indecent or rude or improper language was permitted, evil and ill-disposed persons would have it in their power to use it as a medium of insult to others, and perchance by some accident, such as the crossing of wires, or by a species of induction, the same communication might be launched into the midst of some family circle under very mortifying circumstances."[23]

The Communications Act of 1934 forbids telephoning any comment, request, suggestion, or proposal which is obscene, lewd, lascivious, filthy, or indecent.

4.4 Regulation and monopoly.

4.4.1 The telephone system attests to the efficiency of certain kinds of monopoly. (Type B)

The general American ideology and legal tradition is against monopoly. During the first two decades of the century, when the independents were trying to establish themselves in the telephone field, numerous diatribes against the Bell monopoly were published. One pamphlet, Paul Latzke's *A Fight With An Octopus*[24] was printed in the millions of copies.

Nonetheless, the advantages of an interconnected grand system were conspicious and lent support to the theory of natural monopoly. The 1920s were a time when various doctrines of planning were being disseminated both in the U.S. and in Europe. They affirmed the efficiency of large scale scientific management. The argument in favor of planning cut across the then much more hotly debated issue of public vs. private ownership. Proponents of planning and large scale management were to be found in the early 20th century on both sides of the socialist-capitalist debate. The telephone system was often cited as an example of how a well managed giant monopoly could be efficient and meet public needs.[25]

4.4.2 A privately owned telephone system will be subjected to government regulation. (Type C)

Vail recognized that a corollary of being allowed to have a private monopoly was acceptance of government regulation. He did not fight it; he encouraged it. "The public . . . has begun to appreciate and believe that the telephone service is a natural monopoly; that any telephone exchange must have universal service—from every exchange and every subscriber as a centre in every direction to the farthest talking limits; that one telephone system is sufficient, and more than one a nuisance."[26]

Vail saw regulation as a means to the creation of a single unified system. "Far from opposing public supervision and control," wrote Sydney Brooks in 1912, Vail "welcomes it. He insists that just as 'corporate organizations and combinations have become a permanent part of our business machinery,' so public control or regulation of public-service corporations by quasi-judicial commissions has become a permanent part of our political machinery."[27] "State control or regulation" Vail said "should be of such a character as to encourage the highest possible standard in plant, the utmost extension of facilities, the highest efficiency in service, rigid economy in operation and to that end should allow rates that will warrant the highest wages for the certainty of return on investment."[28]

The regulation of telephony was only part of a general movement in the first four decades of the century for public control over public utilities and natural monopolies, but the large growth of the Bell System was an important stimulus to that movement. And, as with radio broadcasters later, the industry's encouragement of the process was a major factor in bringing about regulation.

4.5 The telephone in politics.

> It is time for someone to write a book, or at least an article, on "The Telephone in Politics." The telephone alone has made it possible for one man to manage a campaign over an entire city. It has curtailed the functions and responsibilities of a district manager as the cable has those of an ambassador. It enables a canvass to be made, or a list of distinguished signatures secured for some "call" or manifesto, without the expenditure of several days' time or the employment of a large corps of workers.[29]

Those words appeared in *Telephony* magazine in 1906. It is still true that no comprehensive study of the telephone in politics has been published.

Implicit in the 1906 statement was a focus on a particular use of the telephone in politics (one of three we shall note here), namely the use of the telephone to manage political organizations and campaigns. It also came later to be used for mass campaigning and for sustenance of political machines.

4.5.1 The telephone will facilitate central management of political organizations and campaigns. (Type B)

The first national election in which the telephone played an important role was McKinley's "Front Porch" campaign of 1896. During the Republican St. Louis convention that year, Speaker of the House Reed tried constantly, but in vain, to talk by phone to his friends at the convention. McKinley, however, succeeded in maintaining close communication with the convention hall from his home in Canton, Ohio which was "looped like a Christmas package with important coils of wire" for both telegraph and telephone. A call was placed from the phone booth near the hall when his name was put in nomination, but the connection seemed to be disturbed by "a curious distant hum, which turned out to be the roar of the demonstration six hundred miles away." Throughout the campaign McKinley maintained contact with his organizers by telephone.[30]

In 1904 the plans for the Democratic national convention, also in St. Louis, provided for a 100 phone network in the hall among state delegations, to the rostrum, and to the newspapermen.[31]

By 1910 use of the telephone had moved out onto the campaign trail. One writer on the California gubernatorial election that year, commented, "In a political campaign the telephone is indispensable. Even candidates are not more necessary for a good lively campaign. . . . The work must be done, so (the candidate) must rely on the telephone."

4.5.2 The telephone when widely diffused will be useful for reaching voters. (Type A)

If the phone was used at the turn of the century by politicians to keep in touch with each other, it was not more than a decade later that there were enough phones around to justify trying to influence voters by a telephone canvass. In 1908 in Atlanta a bank of 45 phones and operators was set up in a store, and voters who were pledged to a mayoralty candidate were phoned and urged to vote.[32] In 1911, a phone company executive in Jefferson City, Missouri, organized such a telephone turnout drive for a municipal bond issue, using a bank of 25 phones and operators.[33]

Before radio came on the scene, there were many suggestions for using the telephone network as a broadcast medium.[34] (These will be discussed in section 4.7 on the telephone and the mass media.) For example, in 1913 Woodrow Wilson addressed a dinner in New York by long-distance telephone, and thereafter was innundated with requests for similar speeches. Wilson, however, found that he disliked the phone, and in 1914 sent a letter announcing that he would make no more long-distance speeches. He also instructed the White House operators never to ring him.

If Wilson's rejection of the phone as an instrument of mass communication was partly a matter of personal psychology, the general failure of the phone to be used that way was not. After the mid–1920s there was simply a much cheaper way of doing the same thing, namely radio. Both before then and afterwards, the key fact was that the phone system had not been designed for one-to-many calls, which campaigns need. One-to-one canvassing is indeed used in campaigns but requires much more manpower than does mass communication. The topic of canvassing is one to which we shall return in section 4.6., but canvassing can rarely reach as many voters as cheaply as a true mass medium.

4.5.3 Telephone utilities in cities lend sustenance to political machines. (Type C)

A third political effect of the telephone has by now been largely forgotten. At the end of the 19th century and still in the first years of the 20th century most large American cities were run by graft-ridden political machines. Public utilities of all sorts were their easiest prey. No trolley system, or electric company, or phone company can run without benefit of municipal franchises, permits to dig up streets, and other cooperation from the city government. Thus every new utility that came onto the scene presented a fresh set of opportunities to the political machines. They could demand jobs, side payments, and other favors in return for their favors. Needless to say, many of these relationships are not documented. Some few are. An article in the *Arena* reports on the padding on the payroll by New England Telephone.[35] "Mr. George Dresser," superintendent of construction for NETCO, ". . . admitted that the company had during the last half of 1906 employed ten per cent of their men in the underground construction department who had not rendered services equivalent to their wages and who got on the payroll through political or other influence, . . ." Such deals were what created and sustained the urban political machines of that day.

4.6 Polling, canvassing and fund raising will be easier by phone. (Type A)

The existence of a telephone network with high levels of penetration provides a sampling frame and also a medium for conducting population surveys.

We have already noted the occurrence of telephone political canvassing starting in 1908. The same idea of using the telephone to reach a large sample of the population occurred to people in various fields such as marketing, advertising, research, and religion. In the same year the Chicago Christian Endeavor Union announced a plan to save 100,000 souls within one year by phoning lists of unconverted friends of members.[36]

We noted earlier (2.1.7.2) that in the early years of city planning the telephone company was the best source of data on urban population and demographic trends. The fundamental plans that phone companies drew up were based upon detailed neighborhood information. That information was obtained in part by telephone polls conducted by the operators. Hubbard and Hubbard[37] describe the Los Angeles procedure in which "a battery of telephone girls called everyone in the city."

In the process of conducting and perfecting such research methods, AT&T became a center of sampling theory. If they carried theory into practice they should have realized, however, the fallibility of samples drawn from telephone directories (convenient as they were) at any period before the 1950s. The *Literary Digest* learned that lesson the hard way. The mailing lists for its 1936 questionnaires on the Roosevelt-Landon election were drawn partly from phone books, which had by then become the main directories in the U.S. But phone subscribers were still an affluent subset of the population. It was partly that bias which led the *Digest* to obtain a Republican majority in its poll in that Democratic landslide year.

By now, in the United States telephone canvassing is used by pollsters, politicians, market researchers, advertisers, and salesmen. It is feasible because in the U.S. most people are not offended and are cooperative when a stranger phones on legitimate business, even the business of promotion. In many countries of the world that kind of approach would be impossible because such an unsolicited promotional call would arouse indignation, not cooperation.

Indeed, with the coming of automatic dialers and tape records, resistance to canvassing is growing in the United States. Automatic canvassing machines were starting to burgeon until the advertisers and others who used them discovered strong opposition to them. Indeed a petition was filed with the FCC to ban or regulate such devices. The FCC in 1980 ultimately declined to do so, partly on free speech grounds. It was not clear how to draw an effective line between abuse and proper use of the network. So telephone canvassing continues to grow, limited only by public non-cooperation.

4.7 The telephone and the mass media.

Under this heading we consider two related matters: the use of the telephone itself as a mass medium, and the use of the telephone by other mass media.

4.7.1 The telephone will (will not) be a means of mass communication. (Type A)

When the telephone was first invented, implicit in the thinking of its promoters were two not wholly compatible theories about its prospective use. One assumption was that the telephone would be used for person-to-person conversations, the other that it would be used as an instrument of mass communication, delivering news, music, entertainment, and information to subscribers. To cite a few early examples of expectations of broadcasting use of the telephone: The *Springfield Republican* observed on February 15, 1877:

> Again, by an instrument skillfully arranged, all the music of a prima donna could be distributed over the country while she was singing, thus popularizing good music to an extent as yet unknown. The Metropolitan newspapers could employ persons to read their articles to subscribers in distant parts . . . Wonderful are the achievements of science, by which the filing of a saw, or the flute playing of an amateur, may be heard round the world like the morning drumbeat of the British army, or the shot fired at Concord Bridge.

In an interview with the *New York Sun* printed five days later, Watson, Bell's assistant, stated that he hadn't the slightest doubt that in a few months a man could lecture in Boston and be heard by an audience in any part of the country. Sidney Aronson describes how for a few a few months Bell himself was initially unsure about this.[38] He then adopted the point-to-point conception described in his 1878 letter.[39] Others persisted for a long time in proposing or experimenting with what Asa Briggs calls "The Pleasure Telephone."[40] In Budapest a service operated from 1893 until after World War I, using a formula much like that of radio today, delivering news, music, financial information, and announcements to subscribers. About 1912 an unsuccessful service of the same sort was established in Newark, New Jersey.[41]

There were various reasons why "the pleasure telephone" failed to take hold. The fidelity of early telephones was poor, but so was the fidelity of early radios and phonographs, so that is not explanation enough. The novelty of these devices overcame any critical perfectionism on the part of the customers. Furthermore, if the demand had existed, the phone system could have been developed toward higher quality sound. That would have been costly, however. High power transmission would have been required so as to override electrical interference and that would have raised the cost of phone service still higher. As it was the telephone was too costly to succeed as a mass medium; that was the determining factor. Two hundred dollars a year at the turn of the century was a feasible payment for a business or a wealthy person. It was not a feasible payment for a worker earning $38.50 a month. (cf, Section 1.1.2). Before electronic distribution of mass communication succeeded (as it did in the 1920s), a device had to be invented that cost the ultimate listener only a fraction of that, even at the higher living standard of two decades later. The radio achieved that cost breakthrough by dispensing with the investment in the wired network. Before radio became economically viable, however, the vacuum tube had to be perfected to the point where the large expensive batteries in early sets could be replaced by wall current.

Part of the economic foundation of most mass communications is advertising. For that revenue to flow there must be enough audience so advertisers will pay their share. It is a chicken/egg problem; the audience must be there to win the advertisers; the ads must be there to serve the medium to the audience. In the case of the introduction of television that dilemma was met by a massive initial investment (mostly by RCA) around 1950. Minimal TV broadcasting had existed since the 1930s, but before the public at large would buy sets, there had to be good programming, and before there could be good programming there had to be sponsors, and before there could be advertising sponsors there had to be mass audience. The log jam was broken fifteen years after TV was technically available, by massive simultaneous investment in broadcasting, software, and promotion of sets, at a vast initial deficit. When that investment was made the country was covered by TV in about four years between 1950 and 1954. If the phone system had had to be introduced in that way there would have been a delay of decades. The problem the phone promoters faced in the 1870s was to find potential users of the new device who would get value from it, even when linked to only one or a few other sets. Businesses or professional people who had to maintain regular communication among limited operating points were thus the natural clients. Starting with initial subscribers to such "intercoms," the phone system could grow gradually and incrementally. The economics thus favored a point-to-point phone system, not a telephonic mass medium.

4.7.2 Use of the telephone by other media.

4.7.2.1 The telephone will speed reporting. (Type A)

In 1880 the *London Times* ran a telephone from the House of Commons to their newspaper office so as to gain half to three quarters of an hour of extra time in reporting late night debates for the morning edition.[42]

The first use of the telephone by a journalist was for a report to the *Boston Globe* of a speech by Graham Bell in Salem, Massachusetts on February 12, 1877. The press was already one of the main users of telegraphy, which had enormously accelerated distribution. It was natural for the press to see the advantage of a medium which permitted a reporter to send in a story without having to carry it in to the telegraph office where the telegrapher would tap it out in Morse code, for another telegrapher to retranslate it back into English at the other end of the line, where it would be handed to a messenger boy for delivery to the newspaper. Reporters had had substantial difficulties with telegraph companies. The most important of these difficulties are not fully relevant here; there had been a struggle between Associated Press and some telegraph companies for control of the function of press wire services. But even on a day-to-day basis there were problems; reporters raced for priority at the telegrapher bottleneck. At an event being covered by many competing papers, the reporters would race to get to the telegrapher first, and indeed sometimes resort to such tricks as tying him up with long messages to delay other reporters. Getting to a phone solved that kind of problem.

Getting to a phone, however, was not always easy in the early days. Phones were not pervasive. One of the problems of a reporter in the field was to find the nearest subscriber and somehow talk or bluff his way into permission to use the phone.[43] In the end, as public call boxes and other phones became widespread, the phone made it possible for papers to get the news from the field almost instantaneously.

4.7.2.2 The telephone changes the relationship of the reporter and editor. (Type B)

It was commonly observed after the telephone had become a commonplace in journalism that it sharpened the division of labor between reporter and editor. The reporter, it was noted, might now stay on his beat and go for weeks without ever coming into the newspaper office. He would phone his stories in to the editor, who would handle them from there on.[44]

4.7.2.3 The telephone system will link network radio broadcasting stations. (Type A)[45]

It was recognized from the beginning of experiments in radio broadcasting, shortly after 1920, that telephone lines could be used to link geographically dispersed transmitters so as to give wider coverage to broadcasts.

This capability was important to the phone company as a source of new business, and also to the broadcasters so each station would not have to create all of its own programs, and it also made broadcasting more attractive to national advertisers.

It turned out that this possibility of networking became the key to resolving a struggle between RCA and AT&T for control of the new medium of radio. The phone company saw radio transmission as a natural extension of telephony, and sought to extend its monopoly into that area too. AT&T developed a plan whereby it would build a transmitter in every community, and make it available for a charge to community institutions for broadcasting; AT&T had no intention of getting into the software field. As an experiment it established WEAF in New York City in 1921. We have already quoted AT&T President Griswold's 1922 assessment, saying if that experiment was commercially succesful stations would be networked by a long lines plant. However, RCA also aspired to dominate broadcasting and had many of the key patents. The outcome was an agreement in which AT&T left the field of broadcasting in return for RCA's commitment to use AT&T lines for networking (i.e., not Western Union's), and the companies agreed on patent licensing between them.

4.7.2.3.1 Networking of broadcasting stations will, in turn, have many social effects. (Type B)

By permitting radio networking, the telephone system has contributed to many of the social effects of national radio (and later TV) such as presidential leadership, national integration, rapid fads, etc.

The first dramatic evidence of the importance of networking was when President Harding died in 1923. Calvin Coolidge's eulogy was carried across the nation by long distance telephone lines to the broadcast stations and thus to an audience of millions. *Telephony* predicted that "this event will mark the broadcasting of presidential messages and addresses over radio as a common feature."[46] Indeed, network radio did lead to just such a growth of presidential power, particularly with Franklin Roosevelt's fireside chats.

But perhaps we are casting our net too widely if we start listing as effects of the telephone all those effects of broadcasting which depend on having a national network. This multi-step process of inference could be continued *ad infinitum*. and produce another book on technology assessment of broadcasting. We will not do that, but will cut the chain of inference here with just the one illustrative example of growth of direct presidential influence. Let us here just note that despite the commitment of Congress to localism in broadcasting (expressed in the Communications Act), thanks to networking we have a national system of broadcasting, with whatever consequences this has had for such matters as national integration or the rapid diffusion of fads and fashions through the media.

4.7.2.4 A result of the failure of the phone company to get control of broadcasting is a technically unsophisticated broadcasting system. (Type A)

One can ask the question, what would have happened if AT&T had been somewhat more aggressive in the research field in the first decade of the century, and had dominated RCA's patent position, and thus been able to implement its broadcasting plan? At least two possible paths of development suggest themselves. One possibility is that the government would not have tolerated AT&T's growing monopoly position and would either have nationalized the system (giving us a state run broadcasting system as in Europe) or broken it up. Alternatively, if the government had allowed AT&T to carry out its plan, there would probably be a broadcasting system quite unlike any in the world today.

Today, phone systems are usually dominated by engineers. but in broadcasting organizations engineers play a rather lowly role. The top positions in commercial broadcasting systems are held by people from either the programming or marketing side, and in government systems by civil servants and producers. The AT&T plan would, however, have made transmission the heart of the business. Since revenue would depend on leasing as much air time as possible, the broadcasters would probably have developed a system with much more efficient use of the spectrum to maximize the number of available broadcast channels, and a pricing scheme allowing for market segmentation so that special interest broadcasters could buy air time without unduly lowering the rates charged to mass broadcasters. If broadcast transmission were placed under rate of return regulation, there would be all the more incentive to invest large amounts in transmission plant to create a high quality and very efficient broadcasting plant. The engineers in charge certainly could have advanced the art far beyond what has been achieved today. On the other hand, the extraordinary development of American programming to maximize mass appeal might have been somewhat less advanced. The present system is designed to maximize the number of people listening and watching, not the number of broadcasters. A common carrier system would be designed to maximize the number of broadcasters, not the number in the audience. Thus there were significant social consequences to the particular outcome of the RCA–AT&T competition.

4.7.2.5 The telephone system will allow feedback for radio talk shows. (Type A)

Another relationship between the telephone and radio is that the telephone network could be used for feedback from the broadcst audience to the head end of the broadcast system. Thus for some kinds of programming such as talk shows or game shows there could be broadcast transmission downstream with the phone system being used for the upstream return. This kind of programming began early in the 1920s and has grown ever since.

4.8 The telephone system will democratize society.
(Type C)

Starting in the 1920s, a contrast was sometimes drawn between mass media (such as broadcasting), which had a tendency to impose authoritative and uniform thinking on society, and the effects of the telephone which lent itself to the spontaneous interaction of individuals. Pound, in his 50th anniversary volume on the telephone said, "Radio broadcasting extends the reach of the public man enormously, but it cannot extend equally the reach of the private citizen. . . . That is why radio's social effects may be justly described as mass efforts, . . . while more intimate means of communication plow their way into the social life, breaking the crust of custom and stimulating new adjustments in every relationship of life."[47] Dilts in 1941 made note of the fact that Hitler had stopped telephone development in Germany by imposing large taxes.[48]

Colin Cherry, Henry Boettinger, and Charles Perry have more recently picked up this theme.[49]Boettinger notes a Stalin quotation of how subversive a telephone system would be to the Soviet system. Cherry stresses the importance of the switchboard in making the telephone system an instrument of democratization. One-to-one or small group intercom systems without switchboards could have provided communication for elite groups. A switched network allows anyone to call anyone. In Section 7.2.1.2.3 we shall note that as telephone penetration grew, use changed from that of a hierarchic device for command to that of an instrument for interactive conversation.

The capacity of the telephone system to allow important people to be called by anyone was viewed in the early days of the telephone as one of its disadvantages, as Perry notes, particularly in England. He quotes A. H. Hastie, leader of the Association for Protection of Telephone Subscribers, commenting in 1898 about complaints of subscribers at being called on trivial matters. "A man might as well complain that he has to open his door to see unwelcome visitors." Hastie's answer was: "The telephone should be primarily answered by a servant" to screen instrusions.[50] It has often been observed that people answer the imperious ring of the phone will talk to people who whom they would not give an appointment. Boettinger and Cherry give some amusing examples including a man in the 1930s who made a hobby of a calling long distance to heads of states.

4.9 The telephone in international relations.

4.9.1 The telephone system will become a global one.
(Type A)

This proposition is a simple extension of Section 1.3's forecast that long distance service would be provided. The first international line went from Paris to Brussels in 1887 and was extended the same year to Amsterdam. For such short distances, however, the international boundary is a technical irrelevancy; if long distance transmission was possible it was clearly possible there. The only issue was whether there was some limit to the length of circuit, short of the circumference of the world. Underwater transmission difficulties might set one such limit, though there was the model of the undersea telegraph cable. In 1891 a Dover-Calais voice cable was laid.

Very long distances however, were only gradually conquered. Local exchanges that would be the basis for a global long-lines system spread rapidly around the world. By the early 1880s there were telephones in service in Cairo, Capetown, Calcutta, Bombay, Rangoon, Colombo, Shanghai, Honolulu, and Buenos Aires.[51] But as we have seen in Section 1.3, until after 1900 the capacity to transmit very long distances did not exist. The Pupin coil, the Marconi experiments with radio, and the De Forest vacuum tube in 1907, along with other inventions, made the difference. By 1915 commercial land line service was opened up from coast to coast in the United States, and experimental radio-telephone calls had been made to Paris and Honolulu. Commercial service from the U.S. to Europe was opened in 1927, from Berlin to Argentina in 1928, from U.S. to Japan in 1934.

While after the turn of the century no one doubted that there would ultimately be a global system, the actual evolution of international lines was often slowed by lack of political incentives for extending lines across frontiers. When the U.S. Signal Corps arrived in Europe in 1917 it found no direct line between Marseilles and London or between Paris and Rome; it installed them.

4.9.2 International telephony will be important in diplomacy. (Type A)

"World-wide facilities for conversation must affect profoundly the relationship of states and peoples."[52] An early dramatic illustration of how important the telephone was to become in international diplomacy was its use at the Washington Conference of 1922. As a promotional effort to get world attention for the conference and to help it succeed, the United States provided unprecedented phone facilities (which, incidentally, left a deep impression on delegates who came from countries where the phone system did not work well). Private lines connected the Navy Building, where the conference was being held, with Conference offices, the Pan American Building, and various foreign embassies. There were over two hundred such lines for the sole use of the conferees. In a city which normally handled 350,000 calls per day, more than 420,000 telephone calls were put through during one record-breaking day of the Conference. The State Department provided the press with free phone service and with special cable connections with the result that the Disarmament Conference got the most complete coverage ever for such an event.

4.9.3 International telephony will favor summitry in diplomacy and reduce the autonomy of ambassadors. (Type B)

Earlier we have noted the tendency of top executives to use the telephone to maintain direct control over what is happening in the field, with resulting reduction of the power of field managers not only in diplomacy, but also in banking and industry (Section 3.1.3). Heads of government or ministers of foreign affairs began phoning their ambassadors in the field with increasingly detailed instructions, and they also started bypassing them entirely, phoning instead to the ministers of foreign affairs or heads of government in other countries, at least in critical circumstances.

In the spring of 1931 world economic conditions had deteriorated to a crisis level. The German government was ready to default on its loans from U.S. banks. After having decided on a moratorium on all war debts as the wisest course of action—a decision reached only after lengthy phone conversations with over thirty leading members of Congress—President Hoover faced the challenge of placating the French government. Because of the urgency of the situation, the President had not even consulted with the French before announcing the planned moratorium on June 21, 1931. The French were outraged upon hearing of Hoover's decision. It was at this point that long-distance telephone diplomacy was used.

According to Hoover's memoirs:

> During this period and subsequent weeks, I was in hourly touch with our representatives in London, Paris, Berlin, and Vienna by transatlantic telephone, and they were in similar close touch with one another. It was the first time that such extensive use had been made of the telephone by our government officials . . . and the telephone afforded far better understanding and much quicker contact than were possible with the slow coding and decoding of formally phrased cables.[53]

The calls were effective, and on July 6, an agreement was signed with the French; but not before having aroused a certain amount of furor in other parts of the world. A June 29 headline in *The New York Times* read, "Phone Diplomacy Arouses Belgians," and the ensuing story read, in part, as follows:

> Belgian politicians are working overtime this weekend on an answer to President Hoover. It transpires that European diplomacy has been abruptly awakened from a centuries-long sleep during the past week by urgent telephone calls from Washington.
>
> Quickly, politicians have realized President Hoover was listening in.
>
> This breach of diplomatic precedent has startled Europe, a Belgian politician declared, relating how Europe was being hustled by new American methods. It is a new world without distances, he said, which makes diplomats feel they have outlived their usefulness when the heads of States can discuss matters almost face to face."[54]

4.9.4 International telephony will foster world peace. (Type B)

In hindsight one can be cynical about this prediction in its more unqualified forms, but in the long run it may turn out that growth of international communication may be a force in that direction. It is easy, however, to find assertions of a fantastically optimistic kind. The same sorts of statements were made about the international cable, long before the telephone. When President Buchanan and Queen Victoria exchanged congratulatory messages by cable in 1858, a newspaper wrote:

> Tomorrow the hearts of the civilized world will beat in a single pulse, and from that time forth forevermore the continental divisions of the earth will, in a measure, lose those conditions of time and distance which now mark their relations.[55]

A poet wrote:

Lo the golden age is come!
Light has broken o'er the world.
Let the cannon-mouth be dumb,
Let the battle-flag be furled;
God has sent me to the nations
To unite them, that each man
Of all future gneerations
May be cosmopolitan.[56]

In similar vein some decades later Gen. Carty wrote:

> Some day we will build up a world telephone system making neces-sary to all peoples the use of a common language, or common understand-ing of languages, which will join all the people of the earth into one brotherhood.
>
> There will be heard, throughout the earth, a great voice coming out of the ether, which will proclaim, "Peace on earth, good will towards men."[57]

4.10 The telephone and warfare.

Whether or not the telephone helped prevent war, it was certainly useful in conducting it.

4.10.1 The telephone will be useful for command and control. (Type A)

The war in which field telephones first made their mark was the

Russo-Japanese War of 1905. Casson describes how the Japanese troops in a crescent 100 miles long moved forward stringing telephone wires behind them, running from each regiment and battery to divisional headquarters. The fifteen divisional headquarters were wired to three group headqarters, and these were wired in turn to General Oyama who sat ten miles behind the line and sent his orders. The Japanese victory was attributed to this communication feat.[58]

The idea may have come to the Japanese by observing the Boxer Rebellion of 1900. The Western troops marching from Tientsin to Peking strung telephone wire behind them. Ater the supression of the rebellion that wire was left in place, providing the first telephone service for China outside of Shanghai.

4.10.2 The telephone encourages centralization of command at higher echelons. (Type B)

This is the same phenomenon that we have already observed with regard to bankers, industrialists and ambassadors (cf Sections 4.9.3, 3.1.3). The example of General Oyama just cited serves to make the point.[59]

FOOTNOTES

[1] Pound. *The Telephone Idea*, p.25.

[2] Pound. *The Telephone Idea*, p. 25.

[3] The Telephone Voice, *Telephony* 6, June, 1906, *11* (6), 382.

[4] Frank Hall Childs. When the Telephone Was Young in Washington, D.C., *Telephony*, April 1, 1933, 104 (13) 17.

[5] Kenneth E. Davison. *The Presidency of Rutherford B. Hayes*. Westport, Conn.: Greenwood Press, 1972, p. 171.

[6] Casson. "The Social Value of the Telephone," p. 899.

[7] Walden Fawcett. How Uncle Sam Uses the Telephone, *Telephony*, Jan. 22, 1910, *18* (4), 89–90; *Telephone Engineer*, Vol. 5, No. 6 June 1911, p. 319.

[8] Telephones in Big Government Building, *Telephony*, Vol. , No. Jan. 23, 1932, 102 (4) p. 18.

[9] Leila Sussman. *Dear F.D.R.* Bedminster Press, Totowa, NJ (1963).

[10] The Telephone in Politics, *Telephony*, Dec. 1906, *12* (6), 364.

[11] Cf. sections 10.5 and 11.3.

[12] Attorney General v. Edison Telephone Co. 6 O.B. Div. 244.

[13] Anon. 10 *Central Law Journal* 178 (1880); William G. Whipple, 22 *Central Law Journal* 33 (1886); W.W. Thornton, 33 *Am. Law Register* 327 (1886); Herbert Kellog, 4 *Yale Law Journal* 223 (1884).

[14] Chesapeake and Potomac Telephone Co. v. Baltimore and Ohio Telegraph Co., 66 Md. 339.

[15] Richmond v. Southern Bell Telephone and Telegraph Co., 174 US 761, 1899.

[16] Ibid.

[17] Cf. quotation in section 1.4.3.5.

[18] *American Law Review* 1885, *33*, 448.

[19] Globe Printing Co. v. Stahl 23 Mo. App. 451, 458, 1886.

[20] E.g., Bank of Yolo v. Sperry Flour Co., 141 Cal. 314, 1903; Young v. Seattle Transfer Co. 33 Wash. 225, 1903.

[21] Brutus Clay. *Virginia Law Review* 337–360. Feb. 1914, Vol.I, No. 5 "The liability of a Telephone Company for Its Negligent Failure to Furnish Promptly Service for Summoning a Physician in Case of Sickness".

[22] 283 US 697, LEd 1357, 51 S Ct 625.

[23] Cf. William H. Rockel. "The Law Relating to Telephones" *American Law Register*, Feb. 1899, *12*, 73 Huffman v. March Mutual Tel. Co, 143 Iowa 590, 1909.

[24] Paul Latzke. *A Fight with an Octopus*. Chicago: The Telephony Publishing Co., 1906.

[25] Cf. Brooks. The Politics of American Business, pp. 708–720.

[26] Public Utilities and Public Policies, p. 318.

[27] Brooks. The Politics of American Business, p. 715. Cf. The Telephone and Government Regulation, *The Outlook*, 1908, 846–47; Casson, "The Future of the Telephone."

[28] Vail. Public Utilities and Public Policies, p. 318.

[29] Telephone in Politics, *Telephony*, December 1906, *12* (6), 364.

[30] *The New York Times*, June 17, 1896. p. 2; H. Wayne Morgan, *William McKinley and His America*. Syracuse: Syracuse University Press, 1963, p. 218; Margaret Leech, *In the Days of Mckinley*. New York: Harper & Brothers, 1959, pp. 81–82.

[31] "Democratic National Convention will Be Conducted By Telephone, *Telephony*, May 1904, *1* (5), 345:, Programme of Convention, Part 1 *The New York Times*, July 6, 1904, p. 1; Telephones At A Convention *Telephony*, Vol. 8, No. 1, July 1904, *8* (1), 34. on reaching newsmen see also The Telephone in The Political Campaign in Oklahoma, *Telephony*, Oct. 24, 1908, *16* (11), 424.

[32] Telephone Aids in a Local Election, *Telephony*, April 24, 1909, *12* (17), p. 493. In Des Moines, Iowa, earlier in the same year a bipartisan turnout drive was organized. with the cooperation of the local phone company (Telephone Help Election Day *Telephony*, June 1908, *15* (6), 373–74). In Kansas in the same year phone calls were made to attract audiences to political speeches (Using the Telephone in Kansas for Political Purposes *Telephony*, Oct. 3, 1908, *16* (8), 324). As early as 1905 it was suggested that the telephone could be used to quell rumors (Bergengren, The Far Flung Telephone, pp. 65–71.)

[33] Percy G. Robinson, Campaigning by Wire, *Telephony*, Nov. 26, 1910, *59* (22), 625; *Telephony*, May 1904, *7* (5), 347; Warren H. James, A Telephonic Canvas for Votes, *Telephone Engineer*, Vol. 6 No. 5 Nov. 1911, pp. 257–8.

[34] For example, playing a record of a campaign speech over the telephone (*Telephony*, Oct. 3, 1908, *16* (8), 338–39).

[35] The Phantom Labor Brigade; or How the New England Telephone and Telegraph Company Squanders the people's Money to Control the political Situation, *Arena*, September, 1907, *38*, 329–31.

[36] Saving Souls By Telephone, *Telephony*, July 1, 1911, *61* (1), 2.

[37] Hubbard and Hubbard. *Your Cities Today and Tomorrow*, p. 93.

[38] Aronson. Bell's Electric Toy, p. 21–22

[39] Pool. *The Social Impact of the Telephone*, pp. 156 5,.

[40] Briggs. The Pleasure Telephone, p. 40. Cf. Edward Bellamy. *Looking Backward.* Boston: Ticknor, 1887.

[41] *Literary Digest,* vol. 44, March 16, 1912, pp. 528–29; Arthur F. Colton. The Telephone Newspaper. *Telephony,* March 30, 1912, *62* (13), 391f; The Budapest News Telephone Telephone. *Telephony,* March 13, 1909, *7* (11), 312; News Service By Telephone. *Telephony,* Nov. 1906, *12* (5), 297. Various experiments were conducted in giving speeches by phone to an assembled audience. Cf. The Telephone As an Entertainer. *Telephony,* May 18, 1912, *62* (20), 610; Campaign Speeches By Telephone. *Telephony,* Oct. 3, 1908, *16* (8), 338 f. Election returns by phone were often mentioned in *Telephony:* Oct. 24, 1908 *16* (11), 423; Campaigning by Wire Nov. 26, 1910, *59* (22), 626; Dec. 16, 1911, *61* (25), 752; Nov. 9, 1912, p. *63* (19), 770; Nov. 16, 1912, *63* (20), 763.

[42] *London Times,* May 17, 1880, p.3.

[43] Use of Telephone By Reporters, *Telephony,* July 1905, *10* (1), 62.

[44] Cf. Casson, The Social Values of the Telephone.

[45] Cf. sections 1.4.5.2 and 8.1.4.

[46] *Telephony,* Dec. 15, 1923, p. 18.

[47] Pound. *The Telephone Idea,* p. 50. Cf. Arthur Page. Social Aspects of Communication Development, 6, 18.

[48] Dilts. *The Telephone in a Changing World,* p. 47.

[49] Cherry. The Telephone System, pp. 124–125; Boettinger. Our Sixth-and-a Half Sense. p. 203; Perry. The British Experience 1876–1912, pp. 77–78.

[50] A.H. Hastie. The Telephone Tangle and the Way to Untie It. *The Fortnightly Review,* 1890 *70,* p. 894.

[51] Dilts. *The Telephone in a Changing World,* p. 38.

[52] Pound. *the Telephone Idea,* p. 52.

[53] Robert H. Ferrell. *American Diplomacy in the Great Depression. Bloomington, Ind.: Archon Books, 1969, pp. 106–15.*

[54] Herbert Hoover. *The Memoirs of Herbert Hoover.* New York: The Macmillan Company, 1952. p. 72. *The New York Times,* June 28, 1931, p. 1; June 29, 1931, p. 10.

[55] Dilts. *The Telephone in a Changing World,* p. 19; cf. How Uncle Sam Uses the Telephone. *Telephony,* Jan. 22, 1910, *9* (4), 91.

[56] Dilts. *The Telephone in a Changing World,* p. 20.

[57] Dilts. *The Telephone in a Changing World,* pp. 188–89. A more modest forecast by William F. Ogburn in *Technology and International Relations.* Chicago: University of Chicago press, 1949, was that the contact inventions, among which he included the telephone, would reduce international heterogeneity (p. 10).

[58] Casson. The Social Value of the Telephone, pp. 904–905. Cf. The Indispensible Telephone. *Telephony,* Nov. 1906, *12* (5), 296; Action at a Distance, *17,* p.39.

[59] Cf. Westrum, *The Historical Impact of Communication Technology on Organization, p. 7;* Albert Speer. *Inside the Third Reich.* New York: Macmillan, 1970, p. 304, on Hitler's control of the field.

5

The Telephone in Emergency Services

5.1 The telephone will promote a sense of security. (Type C)

Wurtzel and Turner analyze a situation long after the period we are studying, namely a fire in a telephone exchange that occurred in 1975.[1] They interviewed residents of an area of lower Manhattan where telephone service was knocked out for three weeks. They found a decided increase in anxiety, particularly about not being able to *receive* phone calls. The respondents knew that they themselves were all right, so they did not worry about not being able to phone out, but since they normally relied on the telephone to inform them if anything happened to loved ones who were not at hand, they worried about not being able to receive incoming calls.

While we have no such rigorous data from the period that we are studying, casual observations about the phone as a source of reassurance were made innumerable times. Most often the comments were made regarding farmers (cf Section 2.2.1.2). Observations were also made regarding housewives left in the suburbs when their husbands commuted to work.[2]

5.2 The telephone will be used for rapid mobilization of a variety of emergency services. (Type A)

A number of examples of types of emergencies were commonly cited.

5.2.1 Floods. (Type A)

Casson[3] cites an operator who drowned staying by her switchboard to warn her customers.

5.2.2 Forest Fires. (Type A)

Many references could be cited.[4]

5.2.3 Coast guard and frontier services. (Type A)[5]

Again, citations referring to the use of the telephone for such purposes are common.

5.2.4 Weather warnings. (Type A)[6]

Dilts notes that the weather bureau warns the phone company of impending storms, so more operators can be put on duty to handle the extra emergency traffic.[7] Numerous sources cite situations in which farmers saved their crops thanks to weather alerts. Dilts tells of California citrus growers having plugs for portable phones out in their fields so as to receive notice of impending frosts.[8]

5.2.5 Fire prevention. (Type A)

In the past most fire fighting systems relied primarily on telegraphic signalling and only to a limited degree on the telephone. The location of the fire was crudely encoded in the alarm signal. Because firemen worked as a team and consistently returned to the fire station after a call, there was no need for a two-way point-to-point communications network (except for a fire squad wanting more assistance). The telephone operator did not serve to organize the fire company since they already had strong internal organization.

By the time the telephone fire alarm system made its debut in 1878 in Burlington, Iowa, its telegraphic counterpart was 27 years old and in use in 75 major cities and towns. District telegraphs, which sent coded messages summoning messengers, policemen, and doctors as well as acting as fire alarms, had been in use in private homes for at least eight years. Various ideas for telephonic fire alarms were promoted, for example in Paris in 1893,[9] and the U.S. in 1905[10] and 1920[11] but failed to take off. In particular, use of the regular switched network suffered from the fact that 24-hour service was not provided as a regular practice until about 1914. The need for it had been recognized as early as 1884.[12] The telephone, when it appeared in fire alarm systems, was mostly an appendage for use by firemen to call headquarters. On the British Isles in the 1930s, fire alarm boxes were telegraphic with telephone jacks. Double-headed boxes were quite popular, with police or ambulance alarms on adjacent boxes to the fire alarm.

If one asks why, in the United States, telephone companies did not design systems better adapted to the needs of municipal fire fighters, and proselytize for that business, the answer seems to be that municipal customers offered far less profit than commercial ones. To win the former took politicking and graft; also, payment for service was less prompt than on the private market.

5.2.6 Crime and law enforcement.

At least from the turn of the century, the telephone was seen as useful to both the police and criminals. Usually it was not the same authors who saw both points.[13] Criticis of the telephone stressed its use in crime; enthusiasts stressed its use in crime prevention.

5.2.6.1 The telephone will improve law enforcement.
(Type B)

In their most enthusiastic statements commentators sometimes forecast that the telephone would so tip the balance between "hunters" and "hunted" that the problem of ordinary crime would virtually be solved.[14] A villainous anarchist, in a 1902 short story, connects a bomb to a phone to be detonated by his call. But in the happy ending, the bomb is detached seconds before he rings; the police trace his call and catch him.[15] Not until late in the nineteenth century did the police make professional use of the telephone. V. A. Leonard offered as an explanation the lax organization of police departments during the 19th century and the self-image of a police officer as a free agent rather than a member of a team. He writes in a book entitled *Police Communication Systems:*

> The need for a complex communication system which would serve as the central nervous system of a highly integrated organism for the suppression and prevention of crime was not perceived until after police organizations began to move from under the rigid control of political officials. With the introduction of some civil service reform and the consequent development of the idea that police work was a specialized profession, police communication began to receive the attention it deserved.[16]

The United States did not take the lead in the area of police call boxes.[17] By the early 20th century, telephones were appearing in police signalling systems abroad. Rio de Janeiro had a complicated system by 1908. Citizens were authorized to purchase keys that would allow them to call for assistance from any of the call boxes. An officer at the police station received the telegraphic signal (much like a fire alarm signal) and transmitted it to the nearest police post. At the police post, a gong sounded the call box number and the number appeared on a sign. Six policemen and a car were then dispatched to the scene of the alarm. By using another key, policemen had access to an inner box with a dial telegraph and telephone at their disposal. The dial telegraph permitted them to set a pointer to a legend on the dial indicating an accident, a fire, and so forth. The telephone was used to communicate directly with any point in the alarm system, and often by headquarters to give instructions to a patrolman—again signalling him with a light or bell. In 1913, a *Scientific American Supplement* carried an article on a Berlin system in which contact boxes were installed on the streets 300-400 meters apart.[18] Every policeman carried with him a telephone jack the size of a watch. Access to the contact boxes required a key. The police department had its own switchboard, which was tied into the municipal system, so the policeman could call not only the district station but also anywhere in the general telephone system.

In the United States, as the telephone gained popularity among police departments, a rival mode of communication emerged—the radio. In 1915, one police department was experimenting with a radio telephone and telegraph set that attached to a motorcycle like a sidecar, and had a transmitting power of one kilowatt.

One major role of the telephone in police work is for citizen reporting of crimes.[19] A 1931 New York City Police Department campaign urged citizens to use the telephone to give information to the police department. Information on criminals could then be broadcast over police radio. Nonetheless, by 1938, Leonard wrote:

> Because of the dual advantage of telephone communication . . . its adaptability to police uses . . . and its instant convenience for calls from citizens . . . telephone service in the modern police department has come to be the very backbone of its communication system. It carries most of the communication load, as it should.
>
> In the setting up of a telephone system, the primary problem is one of economic selection—how to do the satisfactory thing at the lowest cost.[20]

Hindsight induces a jaundiced view of those forecasts which saw the telephone as defeating crime. Such prognoses, we should note, were not made by developers of the telephone system, nor by law enforcement experts, but rather by journalists and reformers. Yet let us not be too complacent about our hindsight. Why were the forecasts that the telephone would significantly reduce crime wrong? Even with all the advantages of hindsight, it is hard to say. *A priori*, it seems sensible that an instrument permitting well organized, dispersed police agents to make contact and warn each other about suspects much faster than the suspects could move should make things harder for lawbreakers. Yet crime increased in the same years that the telephone became available to the authorities; this tells something about the limits of social forecasting based on assessment of one isolated technology. To understand the anomaly of growing crime in the same period as improved technologies of law enforcement, one must understand such matters as the public's attitude toward minor crime, the judges' behavior in sentencing, the organizational incentives in the legal process, the social structure of migrant and ethnic groups in the society, and the nature and reliability of crime statistics.

5.2.6.2 Telephone crime will become a problem. (Type B)

The earliest full scale statement that we have found is an article by Josiah Flynt in 1907 on "The Telegraph and Telephone Companies as Allies of the Criminal Pool Rooms." Flynt charges:

> Because they are among the country's great "business interests." because the stock in them is owned by eminent respectables in business,

and because they can hide behind the impersonality of their corporate existence, they have not been compelled to bear their just share of the terrific burden of guilt. But they have been drawing from five to ten million dollars a year as their "rakeoff" from the pool rooms. . . . Every one of the estimated four thousand pool-rooms throughout the United States is equipped with telephones used for gambling purposes and for nothing else.

Flynt charges that 2% of the New York Telephone company revenues, a million dollars a year, were derived from gambling in pool rooms. He rejects the argument that the phone company should not attend to what subscribers say on their lines; the company, he says, knows full well who the criminal users are, but simply does not wish to forgo the profits of sin.[21]

Prohibition coincided with the telephone system's years of evolution to a national network and total penetration. The bootleggers and the rackets made full use of whatever was available to run their operations;[22] it is hard, however, to take seriously the argument of causality—that somehow there would have been less crime without the telephone.

Other writers deal with telephone confidence men, use of the telephone by burglers to ascertain whether anyone is at home,[23] and the special telephone crimes of cheating the phone company, wire tapping, and call girls.[24]

The courts in numerous cases took note of the use of the phone in illegal activities and held the phone company justified or indeed obligated to refuse phone service for those. In the case of Godwin v. Carolina Telephone & Telegraph Co. 48 SE 636 (Oct. 18, 1904), the court wrote that "while it is true there can be no discrimination where the business is lawful, no one can be compelled, or is justified, to aid in unlawful undertakings." The court held that the phone company would not be required to provide a phone for a home used as a "bawdy house." The phone company was granted the ability to determine the nature of the use to which the phones would be put. In People ex rel. Restmeyer v. New York Telephone Co. 159 NYS 269 (June 2, 1916), the court held that the police could, once determining that a location was violating the law, ask the phone company to remove the instrument.

5.2.7 Medicine.

Physicians were among the earliest users of the telephone in the United States. For example, in 1877 a Hartford druggist organized a physicians' phone exchange.[25] In those early days when there were few subscribers, groups of people who had a common interest in communicating with each other would tend to subscribe at the same time. Thus in Hartford the initial group were physicians. (A glance at the earliest London telephone book reveals few physicians but many solicitors.) An event that gave the telephone much favorable publicity was a railway accident near Hartford. The exchange was able to mobilize a large team of doctors and horses in great haste.[26]

There were numerous stories of a child's lfie being saved by a quick call to the doctor.[27]

Less common but more significant were statements about how the telephone was changing the practice of medicine.

5.2.7.1 The telephone will aid in physician and ambulance routing. (Type A)

"Imagine the shock to a city's nerves" wrote Arthur Pound in the telephone semi-centennial volume, "if it should awake one morning to find that no doctor could be sought by telephone, if no ambulance could be summoned by telphone to remove the victims of a street accident or train wreck, if no hopsital beds could be reserved and no nurses engaged by telephone."[28]

Doctors travelled continually to obscure places, and, unlike firemen or policemen, lacked a team or headquarters; they typically relied on their families and telephone operators to contact them. For the patient there was previously no reliable way of reaching a physician other than coming to his office at visiting hours. So operators in the 19th century often monitored doctors' movements and kept in touch with them.[29]

There was apparently much ambivalence among physicians about the impact of the telephone on their practice. Some articles said that the telephone saved them needless journeys[30]or that it helped in bad weather or at night,[31] but other articles said that patients with telephones find it easier to rèach the doctor to request a house call, especially at night when they are apt to feel worst.[32]

5.2.7.2 Doctors will increasingly make diagnoses and give advice over the telephone. (Type A)

It took a long time for telemedicine to be accepted as good practice. Many doctors felt it unethical to reach a conclusion without seeing the patient. Also, telemedicine raised serious economic questions for the doctor; it is only in recent years that doctors have started billing for telephone advice, and they often do not do it even today. Yet the convenience of the phone, and the inefficiency of either the physician or the patient taking a trip when all he needs is aspirin and bed, have in the end made telemedicine the rule rather than the exception.

Even if full acceptance of telemedicine came slowly, its occasional practice came early, both in emergencies and in minor cases coupled with logistical obstacles to contact. Anecdotes about such matters are common.[33]

Medicine, unlike fire fighting or crime fighting, is a service where advice may be substituted for the actual presence of a professional. The telephone allowed people to feel that the doctor, or at least his advice, was only as far away as the phone. As people came to rely on the phone to find and query a doctor, it became increasingly important for every doctor to have a telephone in order to maintain his practice.

5.2.7.3 Paramedical telephone counselling services will develop. (Type A)

We find little anticipation of this in the period of our study, although a 1919 story notes that use of the lines had been materially increased by "absent treatment" of patients by Christian Science leaders in Los Angeles.[34] Lester has described the many "hot line" services that now exist, but these are largely a post World War II development.[35]

5.2.7.4 The telephone breaks up doctors' neighborhoods. (Type B)

This is a special case of the break-up of single-trade neighborhoods which we have discussed previously (Section 2.1.1). As the *Literary Digest* put it, doctors' "place of congregation now is the telephone book instead of 'doctor's row.' "[36]

5.2.7.5 The break-up of doctors' neighborhoods and the ability to reach established doctors by telephone makes it harder for young doctors to start their practice. (Type B)

The *Literary Digest* article just cited made this point in 1912. Physicians "group themselves in one section or one street, the object being on the part of the new man to possibly receive the call which would have gone to a neighboring physician had that neighbor not been out at the time." With the passing of that symbiotic relationship, young physicians were more on their own.

5.2.7.6 The telephone spreads disease. (Type C)

One common fear in the early day of the telephone was that the mouthpiece, particularly on public phones would harbor germs and spread diseases, especially tuberculosis.[37]

Research was done to assess this danger. The usual conclusion was that the danger was small,[38] though germs might be found in the mouthpieces. Advertisements and articles urged the use of disinfectants on mouthpieces.[39]

We have not been able to establish why this fear has so largely disappeared.[40] Perhaps the reason is habituation, or perhaps the realistic realization that the danger is not large.

FOOTNOTES

[1] Alan H. Wurtzel and Colin Turner. Latent Functions of the Telephone: what Missing the Extension Means. In Pool. *The Social Impact of the Telephone*.

[2] Robinson. *Improvement of Towns and Cities*, quoted in section 9.2.

[3] Casson. The Social Value of the Telephone, p 904.

⁴ Cf. Bergengren. The Far-Flung Telephone, p. 67; Casson, The Social Value of the Telephone, p. 904.

⁵ Cf. Dilts. *The Telephone in a Changing World*, p. 81.

⁶ Cf. section 2.2.1.3.

⁷ Dilts. *The Telephone in a Changing World*, pp. 78–80.

⁸ Cf. The Telephone Exchange, *The Spectator*, September 20, 1879, 52, 1188; Cason. The Social Value of the Telephone, p. 906.

⁹ New Policy Signal, *Scientific American*, Sept. 28, 1895, 73, 204.

¹⁰ Vinton A. Sears (Ed).*Telephone Development: Status of the Industry, Scope and Effect of Competition* (2nd ed). Boston: Banta Press, 1905.

¹¹ A Fire Alarm System Which Telephones Its Message, *Scientific American*, may 1, 1920, 122, 494.

¹² AT&T. *Events in Telephone History,*Sept. 1974, PE/109, p. 11.

¹³ But see Crime and the Telephone. *Telephony*, March 27, 1909, 17 (13), 377, which notes both.

¹⁴ Cf. Dilts. *The Telephone in a Changing World*, pp. 82, 177.

¹⁵ Lawrence Vanzile. Revenge By Telephone. *Telephony*, Sept. 1902,4 (3), 128–9. Cf. Edgar Wallace. *Four Just Men*. London: Tallis Press, 1909; non-fiction treatments in Bergengren. p. 69; The Telephone As a Detective. *Telephony*, Dec. 1907, 14 (6), 351; Heroism13 (1), 36.

¹⁶ V.A. Leonard. *Police Communication Systems*. Berkley: University of California Press, 1938, p. 6.

¹⁷ Although police departments had subscribed to telephones ever since the Washington department took 15 in 1878, they did not deploy them to the beats. On July 20, 1886 the *New York Tribune* ran an editorial criticizing the New York police for not doing what the Brooklyn police had done, connecting the stations with the central office by telephone. The *Tribune* remarked that "doubtless the time may come when every patrolman's beat will be furnished with one of these instruments." Cited in Leonard, *Police Communication Systems*, p. 10.

The Chicago department had been the first to move in that direction. Between 1880 and 1893 over 1000 street boxes were installed. The popularity of such systems received a boost in 1889 when a murderer was caught at the railroad station a few hours after all police in the city had been notified of his description by the phone network.

An article on call boxes, New Police Signal, appeared in *Scientific American*, 1895, 73, 204.

¹⁸ A. Gradenwitz, "German Police Telephone," *Scientific American Supplement*, January 25, 1913, 75, p. 61.

¹⁹ In the heyday of the independent phone companies, one of their selling points was to allow free emergency calls from coin boxes, because many of them used deposit-after-connection devices. They attacked the inhumanity of the Bell System's nickel-first device which could prevent an emergency call if one did not have a coin available. Cf. Emergency Calls, *Telephony*, July 1906, 12 (1), 36; The Unpopular "Nickel First." *Telephony*, Sept. 16, 1911, 61 (12), 324.

²⁰ Leonard. *Police Communication Systems*, p. 52.

²¹ Josiah Flynt. The Telegraph and Telephone Companies as Allies of the Criminal Pool Room. *Cosmopolitan Magazine*, May 1907, 43, 50–57.

² In 1936, the Chief Counsel for the Walker investigation opened his hearings with testimony on the use of the telephone by bookies. Arthur Page, *The Bell telephone System* (N.Y.: Harper Bros., 1941).

²³ Cf. The Burgler and the Telephone. *Telephony*, Aug. 1907, *14* (2), 921.

McLuhan. *Understanding Media*, p. 233 attributes the elimination of red light districts to the call girl and the telephone.

²⁵ Aronson. Bell's Electric Toy, p. 24.

²⁶ Dilts. *The Telephone in a Changing World*, p. 9.

²⁷ E.g., Casson, The Social Value of the Telephone, p. 906; P.C. Henry. A Cooperative Telephone. *Country Life in America*, May 1913, 24, 68: E. E. Free. Few Telephones May Mean High Death Rate. *Literary Digest*, May 24, 1930, *105*, 34.

²⁸ Pound. *The Telephone Idea* p. 39. There were numerous discussions of the usefulness of the telephone when accidents occurred. For example, *World's Work*, December 1913, *27, 237*–38, describes a "Throat Transmitter Telephone" for use in mines to call for help in accidents.

²⁹ Aronson. Bell's Electric Toy.

³⁰ The Telephone in the Medical World. *Telephony*, 1, Jan. 4 1913, *64* (1), 42.

³¹Telephone and the Doctor. *Literary Digest*, May 18, 1912, *99*, 1037.

³² Doctors and Rural Telephone. *Telephony*, June 1905, *9* (6), 492.

³³ Cf. Doctors and Rural Telephone, p. 492; Talking by Wire, *Bristol* (England) *Times*, November 7, 1879, p. 1.

³⁴ The Silent Use of the Telephone, *Telephony*, Oct. 30, 1909, *18* (18), 440.

³⁵ David Lester. The Use of The Telephone in Counseling and Crisis Intervention. In Pool. *The Social Impact of the Telephone*.

³⁶ The Telephone and the Doctor, *Literary Digest*, May 18, 1912, *44*, 1037.

³⁷ Telephonic Germs and the Doctors. *Telephony*, Sept. 1905, *10* (3), 220–29; The Transmitter Mouthpiece and Tuberculosis. *Telephony*, April 27, 1912, *62* (17), 51; A Vest-Pocket Transmiiter for the Telephone. *Scientific American*, Feb. 3, 1912, *106*, 112; H.R. Van Devanter. A Telephone Transmitter without a Mouthpiece. *Scientific American*, May 24, 1913, *108*, 468. Other fears concerned damage to hearing: Is the Telephone Making Us Left-Eared. *Telephony*, July 1904, *8* (1), 74; Telephone Does Not Injure Hearing. *Telephony*, 6, June 1907, *13* (6), 399.

³⁸ Cf. Consumption and the Telephone. *Current Literature*, Nov. 1908, *45*, 571; Telephonic Germs and the Doctors, pp.220–21; and The Transmitter Mouthpiece and Tuberculosis, p. 51.

³⁹ Ventilation of Telephone Booths. *Telephony*, Feb. 1908, *15* (2), 131; Red Cross Telephone Disinfectant. *Telephony*, June 10, 1911, *60* (25), 705–706.

⁴⁰ But not completely. In 1976 the German magazine *Quick* ran an investigative report on dirty coin phones. On examining 250, they said they found germs that could cause bone and kidney inflamations and fatal fungi. (*Asahi Evening News,* Tokyo, December 11, 1976.)

6

The Telephone, Resource Use and the Environment

6.1 Overhead wires are an eyesore.
(Type C)

6.2 Overhead wires are a danger. (Type C)

As the telephone network grew, the wires in the streets became intolerable. Pictures from the time show an enormous mass of wires strung from pole to pole.[1] They not only spoiled the view, they also dripped in a thaw, blocked firemen, and occasionally fell on houses and passers-by. So great was the threat to the environment that in 1880 and 1890 New York City sent axmen to chop down telephone poles.[2]

The phone company recognized the writing on the wall and a great deal of research went into mastering the problem of underground cables, which at first suffered from excessive attenuation. In the end they became the standard solution in built-up areas.

6.3 The increase in the size of the telephone system threatens the depletion of trees. (Type C)

One of the problems frequently discussed in early issues of the trade journal, *Telphony*, was the sources and supply of trees suitable for telephone poles, and their treatment for preservation.[3] As time passed and the system grew, it became apparent that the demand for such trees would exhaust the supply of them. That was one incentive for laying underground cables. Also experiments were run with substitute materials for telephone poles.[4] Incidentally, it was noted in 1936 that the telephone directories were using 25,000 tons of paper a year, but papermaking used different types of trees.[5]

6.4 The increase in the size of the telephone system threatens the depletion of copper supplies. (Type C)

Another problem addressed by research was reducing the thickness of copper wire needed to carry a telephone message. The Pupin coil, for example, contributed greatly to reducing attenuation and thus permitted the diameter of wires to be cut from one eighth inch in 1900 to one sixteenth in 1910. (Cf, Section 1.3).

The copper supply remains, even to this day, a potential problem for telephone system development. Shortages reveal themselves first in the market in the form of price increases. A few years ago, at about the same time as the oil crisis, there was a rapid increase in the price of copper. It was one of the factors that led to great interest in optical fibers. Silver wires are even better than copper, but are obviously too expensive; aluminum wires are inferior. Optical fibres are the likely substitute of choice.

Subsequent to the 1974 run-up, the price of copper collapsed again, removing the pressure, but only temporarily. It is possible that a copper problem may be avoided in the long run only by the widespread use of optical fibers.

FOOTNOTES

[1] Cf. AT&T.*The Telephone in America.* AT&T, 1936, p.33; Edward Mott Wooley. a $100,000 Imagination. *McClure's Magazine,* May, 1914, *43,* 128.

[2] Dilts. *The Telephone in a Changing World,* p. 26.

[3] Cf. To Prolong Life of Telephone Poles. *Telephony,* July 1905, *10* (1), 51.

[4] Hendrick, "Telephones for the Millions," p. 55.

[5] AT&T. *The Telephone in America,* p.36.

7

The Telephone and Complementary Services

7.1 The telephone and the transport industry.

7.1.1 The telephone will help in coordinating trains, traffic, and deliveries. (Type A)[1]

Casson reports that:

> In the operation of trains the railroads have waited thirty years before they dared to trust the telephone, just as they waited fifteen years before they dared to trust the telegraph. In 1883 a few railways used the telephone in a small way, but in 1907, when a law was passed that made telegraphers highly expensive, there was a general swing for the telephone.[2]

The telephone, he claimed, cut the message time in half, and more important, did not require a trained Morse code operator at every location.

We noted previously (section 3.4.3) references to the use of the telephone in the rapid distribution of perishables. In general, the greatest business use of the phone has been in finance, commerce, and where complex logistical coordination is required.

7.1.2 The availability of the telphone reduces the need to travel. (Type A)

Discussion of the communication/transportation trade-off is not new. It was noted early that the telephone could save its user many trips.[3] As we have already noted (3.4.4), the pattern of activity of travelling salesmen changed,[4] and some railroads claimed to be able to feel the resulting decline in their traffic.

That the impact of the telephone in reducing travel was not dramatic is testified to by Casson who says, "slowly and with much effort the public was taught to substitute the telephone for travel."[5]

7.1.3 The telephone increases relationships with people at a distance, thus leading to an increase in travel. (Type B)

In the early literature we have not found examples of this proposition, the opposite of 7.1.2, that is often put forward today.

7.2 The telephone and the post and telegraph industries.

7.2.1 Substitutability.

7.2.1.1 Since phone, post, and telegraph can serve many of the same purposes, whichever is well run will thrive at the expense of the others. (Type C)

Burton Hendrick, among others, noted the difference in development of the different modes in the U.S. and Europe. "The European more often writes or telegraphs; the American more frequently telephones."[6] At that time, he reports, it took 90 seconds to get a suburban connection in New York City, and 30 minutes in London. It is not surprising that at that time 70% of the world's telephones were in the United States. Hendrick also reports rural free delivery at that time served 58,000 communities; the phone served 70,000. By 1911 Western Union's gross was but $38 million compared to AT&T's $179 million.[7] Conversely, in many countries of Europe mail, telegraph, and now telex service are better than in the United States, and, as we noted in the Introduction, are more used.

7.2.1.2 The telephone will cause declines in the post and telegraph systems. (Type B)[8]

While the previous proposition merely noted a competition that could go either way, those who were more optimistic about the prospects of telephony noted that the growth of telephone usage would be partly at the expense of post and telegraph.

That the telephone represented a threat to the telegraph was recognized from the day of the phone's invention. There is a widely believed story that Western Union was so blind to the importance of the telephone that it refused the Bell patents for $100,000, with Orton the President of Western Union remarking, "What use would Western Union have for an electrical toy." The story is largely apocryphal but like most myths continues to be believed because it sounds so "true to life." The correct version can be found in Bruce's standard biography of Bell.[9] There is no substantial evidence that Orton ever said exactly that.[10] It is true that Western Union foolishly rejected an offer of the Bell patents for $100,000—surely one of the worst business decisions of all time. The reason, however, was not an underestimation of the telephone. The reason was that Orton believed that his company could develop telephone service under the Gray and Edison patents and did not need Bell's. An irrational element did enter into that decision: Hubbard, Bell's father-in-law, had been a populist crusader against Western Union's service, promoting a bill in Congress to create a rival postal telegraph system. Orton found the idea of enriching his critic, Hubbard, very distasteful. But he did not doubt the importance of the telephone.

The telephone had a number of advantages over the telegraph.

7.2.1.2.1 Telephoning is faster than telegraphing. (Type A)

Words are spoken at more than twice the speed that they can be tapped out, even by an expert telegrapher.[11] Add to that the time for originally writing out the text, carrying it to the telegraph office, and delivering it to the receiver. We have already noted the time saved by the *London Times* when it installed a phone at the House of Commons.

7.2.1.2.2 The telephone goes end-to-end; it requires no messenger to and from the offices. (Type A)

We have previously noted *Punch's* comments on this and on 19th century efforts to create end-to-end printing telegraphs (cf. Sections 1.1.2; 1.4.1). The nearest to this goal that was widely achieved was installing electric call bells from frequent users to the local telegraph office. When the business had a telegram to send someone would buzz the telegraph office a few blocks away and a telegraph boy would come to pick up the message.

Even today, in places where telephone service is inadequate, the phone is used more for the delivery of commands and messages than for discussion. This author has been engaged in a study of telephone use in Egyptian villages. One of the surprises has been that incoming calls are often not to the ultimate target person, but are instructions and messages dictated over the phone for delivery to the addressee. The point is that there are so few phones in an Egyptian village that the odds are very small of being able to call directly to where the target person is. The caller has to use the phone like a telegraph, as a way of getting his message to an office from where it can be delivered. Only with the growth of a more pervasive phone system did it become a more democratic instrument for two-way interaction.

7.2.1.2.3 The telephone allows two-way interaction in real time. (Type A)

This point, though understood, was discussed surprisingly little in the early days of the telephone. There was instead a tendency at first to anticipate that the phone would be an instrument for hierarchic interactions; giving instructions rather than negotiating and discussing. Cherry notes this and quotes an 1877–78 advertisement describing uses of the phone including communications between "principles and employees," "central and branch banks," "superintendent and his leading men," "manager's office and the employees."[12]

To appreciate why this hierarchic perception was common at first, we must recall that the first subscribers to telephones tended to be business owners who needed to keep control of two or more separated premises. Also, poor fidelity made telephoned words not always easy to understand. It was only when the phone became both more pervasive and also was improved in fidelity that many equals found they could use it to engage in discussion.

7.2.1.2.4 The telephone's labor costs are lower than the telegraph's. (Type A)

A telephone call required only the brief attention of a relatively low-skilled switchboard operator at the beginning and end of the conversation. A telegraph required two highly skilled Morse code operators throughout the transmission.

Telegraphers in that day's labor force were what computer programmers are today. They had a scarce skill which earned them high pay. They had to be bright and quick, but they did not have to come up through any conventional educational or experience channel. It was therefore an ideal job for a highly intelligent non-conformist. But unlike contemporary programmers, they had to locate themselves in isolated remote locations. There they tended to be the local bohemians.[13] In any case they were expensive and sometimes critically missing.[14]

7.2.2 The telephone eliminates jobs for telegraphers. (Type B)

This is a simple corollary of the last point. When railroads, for example, replaced telegraphs with telephones, either telegraphers were discharged or new ones not hired. At local rural stations the station master could handle the phone calls himself. He no longer needed a Morse code operator with him.[15]

In a report on the Philadelphia Centennial Exposition of 1876, at which Bell first exhibited his phone, the *New York Tribune* asked what might be the use of this "curious device." It replied: "There may be occasions of state when it is necessary for officials who are far apart to talk with each other without the interference of an operator"—by which it meant telegrapher.[16]

7.2.3 The telephone and telegraph will form one integrated system with shared lines. (Type A)

This was perhaps an erroneous expectation; it has not happened yet. But with the coming of computer communications there is reason for thinking it may yet happen. The independent telegraph system is declining; it now rents many lines from AT&T and it telephones its telegrams. Computer networks operate over phone lines. Leased lines are multiplexed with voice and teletype. Yet the early attempts to use phone lines for telegraphy, to use telegraph lines for telephones, and to merge the companies were all frustrated, partly by antitrust action and partly by differing technical requirements that made multiple use less attractive economically than it may have seemed at first glance.

In 1892 the Bell System had developed and offered in private line service a simplex method of carrying both voice and telegraph on the same line.[17]

The technical possibility of multiplexing voice and telegraphic code on the same line was shown by Major George Squires of the Signal Corps about 1910. Anticipating acquisition of Western Union, the Bell System had started research on that topic in the previous year.

In 1910 AT&T bought control of Western Union for $30,000,000. Vail had hopes of really creating one universal system.[18]

However, in 1913 federal antitrust action forced divestiture as part of the Kingsbury commitment. Some relations remained between the two systems. Telegrams were accepted by phone.[19] After 1914 AT&T continued in the teletype field, acquiring and merging a couple of companies into the Teletype Corporation in 1929 (which too it was later forced to divest) and offering two-way teletype service as of 1931.[20]

FOOTNOTES

[1] Cf. Telephone Used to Signal Trains. *Telephony*, July 1904, 8 (1), 67; The Telephone in Railway Service. *Telephony*, 6, December 1906, *12* (6), 358–59; The Telephone and Railroads. *Telephony*, June 1907, *13* (6), 369.

[2] Casson. The Social Value of the Telephone, p. 902.

[3] *The Spectator* in 1879(September 20, *52*, 1187–88) predicted that the home phone would be used in place of personal meetings. Cf. Wells. *Anticipations*, pp. 65f.; The Telephone in Modern Business. *Telephony*, Nov. 1901, *2* (5), 190–91; James K. Pollock, Jr. *Party Campaign Funds.* New York: Knopf, 1926, pp. 154–5 (in regard to campaigning); Value of Rural Telephones, *Telephony*, Aug. 1906, *12* (2), 117, and The Farm Telephone, *Telephony*, Jan. 1908, *15* (1), 23 (on saving farmers trips to town.); The *Scientific American* in 1914, Action at a Distance, predicted less transport congestion.

[4] The Telephone in Modern Business. *Telephony*, Dec. 1906 *12* (6), 353.

[5] Casson. The Telephone As It Is Today, p. 12777.

[6] Hendricks. Telephone for the Millions.

[7] Cf. Elbert Hubbard. *OurTelephone Service*. East Aurora, N.Y.: Roycrofters 1913.

[8] Cf. The Telephone and Telegraph. *Telephony*, Sept. 1902, *4* (3), 121; The Telephone Letter. *Telephony*, Nov. 1905, *10* (5), 362.

[9] Bruce. Bell.

[10] Gray once used the phrase "electrical toy".

[11] A telegrapher according to Aronson (Bell's Electric Toy, p. 17) averaged about 25 words per minute.

[12] Cherry. The Telephone System, p. 121.

[13] For a discussion of the character of the telegrapher's way of life, and their rise and fall see W. Fred Cottrell. *The Railroader.* Stanford, California: Stanford University Press 1904.

[14] Bismark introduced the phone into Germany to provide communication to rural post offices too small to afford a telegrapher. (Dilts. *The Telephone in a Changing World,* pp. 11f.)

[15] But cf. G. K. Heyer. The Telephone and the Railroad. *Scientific American,* Supplement, Dec. 17, 1910, *70,* 388–89, minimizing that expectation.

[16] Lally Weymouth. *America in 1876.* New York: Random House, 1976.

[17] Cf. *Events in Telephone History,* p. 11; also Simultaneous Telegraphing and Telephoning. *Scientific American,* June 6, 1904, *90,* 459.

[18] See AT&T Annual Report for 1910 for a statement of that aspiration.

[19] This practice in London was noted by *Telephony* in Sept. 1902. 4 (3), 119.

[20] In 1933, Wiley and Rice, *Communication Agencies and Social Life,* op. cit. (see p. 93 Fn. 58) noted that "modern technology is tending to obscure and even eliminate the customary distinctions between" telegraph and telephone as well as between wired and wireless service, as new hybrid services develop. (p. 146). In present-day commentary this process is referred to as "convergence of modes" and is generally identified as an important current trend.

8

System Development

8.1 The development of a telephone system stimulates research and development. (Type A)

No aspect of the American telephone system deserves more admiration than its scientific research. Bell labs is one of the most creative research organizations of all times. No doubt the superb quality of Bell labs was a result of human choices and not an inevitable result of the phone system; many other countries have telephone laboratories that are more derivative and less creative. Yet they all have labs. Some major push in the direction of research and development (R & D) would seem to have been a necessary result of trying to develop a telephone system.[1] Telephony would grow or not according to its relative efficiency as compared with competitive technologies such as mails, the telegraph, the phonograph, and radio, not to mention new devices in telephony. There were many problems of fidelity, reliability, transmission, and economy to be solved. The very size of a phone system created unprecedented problems of systems analysis. The company size as a unified organization made investment in R & D a profitable use of capital, for the benefits would be appropriated to the company and spread widely over users. Many studies have found that small companies in competitive industries can seldom justify spending the same percentage of income on R & D as large dominant ones.

In addition, in the telephone field the U.S. patent system worked as intended to stimulate R & D at that period. The early history of telephony is in large part a history of patent battles. R & D was largely oriented to "occupying the field" by patents.

Gardiner Greene Hubbard, Bell's father-in-law, and Thomas Sanders, the two men who financed Bell's original work, did so with the intention of acquiring patents that could be quickly and profitably sold. The name of the organization they formed in 1875 was the Bell Patent Association.

When the founders failed to sell their patent to Western Union, they continued the business by issuing franchises. They brought Vail on board and fought off Western Union's rival Edison and Grey patents in the courts. That battle demonstrated the need for continuing research. One measure was the recruitment of Emile Berliner, who offered an answer to the advantages of

Edison's carbon transmitter. In 1879 the Bell interests won their case against Western Union; the latter conceded the validity of the Bell patent, withdrew from the telephone field, and licensed its patents to the Bell System for telephony.

Under Vail the company was reorganized with the acquisition in 1881 of a manufacturing company with its own research staff (Western Electric) and coordination of the system by the instrument of a long lines company (AT&T, formed in 1885) interconnecting the local companies. Research on long distance transmission was given priority even in periods of financial stringency and staff cuts.

Looking forward to the period of competition that would follow the expiration of Bell's fundamental patent in 1893, Vail felt that the company should "occupy the field" by the preemptive development of fundamental technology. However, Vail left the company, not to return until 1907. Management under Stockton, Hudson, and Hammond Hayes was less imaginative and technologically somewhat complacent. Hayes ran a significant research program on practical problems, but except for Campbell's work on long distance transmission, fundamental research, he felt, was better left to be borrowed from Harvard and M.I.T. Also, automatic switching was underestimated.

Between 1894 and 1907 the Bell system's competitors did indeed make several important innovations; particularly in mechanical switching. Pupin's coil anticipated what the company's laboratories were on the way to accomplishing, and his patent had to be bought. When financial control of the AT&T Company changed hands in 1907, the new management persuaded Vail to return to the company. Vail devoted his first efforts upon returning to AT&T to the reorganization of research. The reorganization was extensive and temporarily involved retrenchment.

The Boston laboratory was moved to New York, and its Chief Engineer, Hammond Hayes, was replaced by Vail's close associate, John J. Carty. The operating companies were instructed to discontinue all independent research work and to refer all new apparatus needs to the Engineering Department of the American Company. All inspection activities were assigned to Western Electric. Both funding and staff were cut back sharply (the number of research staff members declined until the summer of 1909). During this period of staff cuts and reorganization most engineering activity was directed towards improved standardization and quality control of apparatus. Carty also began to organize the new "research" sections; but the active development of fundamental research within the American company began only in 1911.

Following the period of retrenchment (1907-summer 1909), Carty organized a new research division. A series of comments by Carty between

1909 and 1911 reflect that the new division was to engage in basic research and that the direction of that research was to be into wireless technology:[2]

> At the present time scientists in Germany, France, and Italy and a number of able researchers in America are at work upon the problem of wireless telephony. While this branch of the art seems at present to be rather remote in its prospects of success, a most powerful impetus would be given to it if a suitable telephone repeater were available. Whoever can supply and control the necessary telephone repeater will exert a dominating influence in the art of wireless telephony when it is developed. (1909)[3]

Both the staff size and research expenditure grew quickly between 1911 and World War I; "In 1910 there were 192 engineers employed in development work, and the expenditures were $493,527. In 1916, there were 959 men, and expenditures amounted to $1,539,621."

But as we have noted in section 4.7.2.3, AT&T started too late to gain control of radio. In the end it had to surrender broadcasting in exchange for exclusive licenses for the wired telephony field.

This experience lay behind the formation of the Bell Telephone Laboratories in 1925. The heads of AT&T had seen how a new technology on the margins of telephony had threatened to create a new competitive system of communication that might have undercut the existing phone system. To try to avoid anything like that happening again, Bell labs was given a wide charter for fundamental research, not just in telephony, but in all the neighboring areas. Out of that research came the transistor, and much of the fundamental work in television, computers, information theory, and innumerable other scientific advances.

We will not try to list systematically all the major scientific and technological advances that came partially out of telephony.[4] What follows is a rather arbitrary noting of some of the most important ones for the period before World War II. Those we list are technologies that in turn had significant social effects that should be noted in our assessment. The forecast, in each case, is that offspring of the telephone would become important to society in some particular uses.

8.1.1 The phonograph. (Type A)

The phonograph, invented by Edison in 1877, was not originally intended by him for its present use as a home music machine. He was working on a device to supplement the telephone by recording messages. We have already discussed the (Section 1.4.3) the various attempts to use the phonograph in connection with telephony.[5] But, while it was never cost effective in its intended use in telephony, it proved enormously successful as a music box.

8.1.2. The loudspeaker. (Type A)

This device was in use by 1916.[6] Before radio broadcasting emerged as a promising prospect, the Bell System devoted considerable research effort to improving public address loudspeaking systems. These would have been important in telephony had use of the phone for entertainment not been pre-empted by radio; at the cost of doing the job by phone, listening might well have become a community activity rather than one carried on in each home.[7]

8.1.3 Sound movies. (Type A)

In 1922 a phonograph record was experimentally synchronized with silent film. The first Vitaphone movie was Warner Brothers' *Don Juan*. Vitaphone was a Western Electric product. A 1926 discussion of it in the *Bell Laboratories Record*[8] takes a rather cautious view of its possibilities. Joseph Maxfield noted that the sound seemed imbalanced and detracted from realism during closeups. Nonetheless, by 1928 there were many sound films, the great majority of them made with Bell equipment; RCA was a distant runner-up.

ERPI, the Bell subsidiary established for the sound motion picture business, became a significant corporate factor in filmdom, so much so that when Hollywood film makers began to have financial problems in the 1930s the Bell System found it necessary to help finance them with rather substantial investments in movie making. Next to the Chase Bank, AT&T was, in the heart of the Depression, the principal funder of the movie industry.

8.1.4 Radio. (Type A)[9]

In section 4.7.2.3 we have traced the relationship of the Bell System with radio, and noted that the pioneering work was done by others such as Marconi and de Forest. However, after 1907 the Bell System made a major effort to catch up and develop the art.

The relationship of telephony to radio was not limited to the direct activities of the Bell System. A more fundamental question is how far the radio idea was influenced by the telephone experience. Our study of telephone development does not provide an answer to that question. At the time of the original work on wireless at the turn of the century, the word used for it was wireless telegraphy, suggesting that the telegraph was the model and the expectation was to send Morse code by pulses through the ether. But it did not take very long in an age when the telephone already existed for people to speculate about the next step, i.e., wireless telephony. Recall that Bell had, as early as 1879, in a paper to the American Academy of Arts and Sciences in Boston, described a selenium radiophone working with light (cf. section 1.4.5.1). The first voice broadcast using radio transmission was made by Fessenden to ships at sea on Christmas Eve 1906. In the first third of the century there was considerable discussion of convergence of modes, not only between wired telephony and wired telegraphy (cf. section 7.2.3) but also between the wired and wireless sytems.[10]

8.1.5 Broadcasting networks. (Type A)

We have noted in section 4.7.2.3 that networking of transmitters was part of the Bell System's conception of a broadcasting system, even at the time of its early experiments in that field (c. 1921). The long lines network has continued as Bell's part of the broadcasting system to this day. Within the past five years the Bell System has begun to lose some of this business to alternative satellite networks.

8.1.6 Telephotos and facsimile. (Type A)

The invention of facsimile preceded the invention of the telephone. Alexander Bain outlined the principles of telegraphic transmission of pictures in a British patent in 1843. Giovanni Caselli conducted experiments from 1863 to 1868. A French commercial effort was made in 1865. In 1875, a year before the telephone, William Sawyer made a breakthrough in better methods, and Arthur Korn made another breakthrough with a selenium cell optical scanner in 1902. Bell System research also played a role in advancing the art of sending graphics by wire to a practical and widely used one. In 1903, Lockwood, of the company's research staff, issued a report on telephotography, pointing out the many technical difficulties, but evidencing the company's interest.

By 1910 there was a regular news picture service among London, Paris, and Berlin. By 1925 telephotos were important in journalism.

8.1.7 Television and videophone. (Type A)

From the time of the invention of the telephone, the idea occurred to many people that if a voice could be captured and sent over wires, transmission of pictures was an obvious next step. The difficulties in going from conception to realization were frequently underestimated by non-technical people. The more naive and less scientifically sophisticated the writer, the more immediate the extrapolation from telephone to television seemed.

Kate Field, a British reporter associated with Bell, projected in 1878 that eventually, "while two persons, hundreds of miles apart, are talking together, they will actually *see* each other!"[11] That belongs in a class of jouranlistic whimsy along with the *Chicago Journal* suggestion:

> Now that the telephone makes it possible for sounds to be canned the same as beef or milk, missionary sermons can be bottled and sent to the South Sea Islands, ready for the table instead of the missionary himself. [12]
>
> In 1879, in *Punch,* the artist George Dumaurier . . . showed two people by a fireplace, watching a sporting match on a screen above the mantle. Sounds were transmitted by telephone. [13]

In 1902, Fawcett in "Successors of the Telephone," reported one of what was to become a long series of claims to have invented television, a device called by its "inventor," Philip K. Stern, a teloptoscope.[14] In 1906 an issue of *Telephony* noted the invention by J.B. Fowler of the televue. Tested over a distance of 6,000 feet it could reproduce a picture of a scene placed in front of it including the colors of the objects in the picture.[15] Fowler felt that he would revolutionize the art of telephony, but the manner in which he foresaw this, though it included entertainment, was divergent from what would occur first when the television was finally put to use.

> Mr. Fowler confidently predicts that he can construct an instrument that will enable a train dispatcher (sic) to see all the trains on his division at one time, note their movements from one terminal to another, and therefore be far better able to prevent disastrous wrecks. The merchant can sit in his home and by utilizing this unique telephone see the interior of his store and watch the conduct of his clerks during his absence. Deaf mutes can carry on a conversation in the sign language over the televue and women can do their shopping by means of the instrument. . . . From this it is only a step to the time when a physician will use the televue to scrutinize a patient's tongue at long distance and then prescribe the necessary medicine over the wire.[16]

With these possibilities unfolding, it is no little wonder that the editorial in that issue of *Telephony* asks, if seeing and hearing are now possible on the telephone "will these two lead to the tasting and smelling and feeling telephone?"[17] In 1910, Casson made a passing comment in an article on "The Future of the Telephone," to the effect that "there may come in the future an interpreter who will put it before your eyes in the form of a moving-picture."[18] A more serious discussion of "The Future Home Theater" by Gilfillan, appeared in 1912. In some respects it is a remarkable forecast, in others a dismaying one.

> There are two mechanical contrivances . . . each of which bears in itself the power to revolutionize entertainment, doing for it what the printing press did for books. They are the talking motion picture and the electric vision apparatus with telephone. Either one will enable millions of people to see and hear the same performance simultaneously, . . . or successively from kinetoscope and phonographic records. . . . These inventions will become cheap enough to be . . . in every home. . . . You will have the home theatre of 1930, oh ye of little faith.[19]

Gilfillan believed that both the cable and over-the-air form of video broadcast would coexist by 1930, and also that there would be a television of abundance with libraries of recorded material from which one could choose. He thought great art would drive out bad; he described an evening program of Tchaikovsky, ballet, Shakespeare, educational lectures, and a speech by a presidential candidate on "The Management of Monopolies." He thought that the moral tone of the home theatre would be excellent. And he maintained that the difficulties in having all this were not technical but human.

By 1927 the Bell Laboratories demonstrated TV on telephone wires between New York and Washington, D.C., and over the air between New York and New Jersey.

President Walter Gifford of AT&T readily admitted that the elaborateness of the equipment required by the undertaking "precludes any present possibility of television being available in homes and office generally." For what, then, would television be used? Gifford could only say:

> What its practical use may be I shall leave to your imagination. I am confident, however, that in many ways and in due time it will be found to add substantially to human comfort and happiness.[20]

Following the first public demonstration of two-way television, Dr. F. B. Jewett, President of Bell labs, predicted further use, but felt that the wide transmission band, the high use of electrical power, and so forth would make television both difficult and expensive. Three years later President Gifford repeated that. "The future commercial possibilities of television are still uncertain."[21]

Two years later the *Bell Telephone Quarterly* again attempted to look at the future of television. Herbert Ives examined the cost of a channel and other economic considerations.

> In image transmission for purposes of entertainment, . . . the element of simultaneity, which pertains to television in its strictist interpretation, is probably not necessary. . . .
>
> If instead of carrying the motion picture film from place to place,

motion pictures could be transported electrically by a television system.
the choice between the use of a home motion picture projector and a television apparatus receiving film images from a broadcasting station would
depend entirely on the question of cost and convenience. [22]

To Ives, whether recording of the television picture was done on-line or
off-line was unimportant, for the need for real time simultaneity was not
apparent.

In the early 1930s AT&T installed TV phone booths to test the market
for commercial videophone service.

By 1938, when the Walker investigation of the telephone industry
published its report, television already existed but had not yet reached the
general public. The Walker Report projected two ways it could develop:

> Television offers the possibility of a nation-wide visual and auditory
> communication service, and this service might be developed under either
> of two broad methods. The first is by the eventual establishment of a series
> of local television broadcasting stations similar to the present local radio
> broadcasting stations . . . or conceivably it may develop into some form of
> wire plant transmission utilizing the present basic distributing network of
> the Bell System, with the addition of coaxial cable or carrier techniques
> now available or likely to be developed out of the Bell System's present
> research on new methods of broadband wire transmission. [23]

The one forecast the report did not make, and which now seems the
most plausible, is that over time it would go first one way and then the other.
With time unspecified, both forecasts may be realized.

8.1.8 The telephone network will become a teletype network too. (Type A)

In section 1.4.1 we noted the long history of alphabetic printing
telegraphs going back long before the telephone. While these are in no way the
offspring of the phone, the two technologies are so akin that repeated efforts
have been made to put the two services onto one set of lines. Until recently,
however, anti-trust policy prevented that from happening. The Kingsbury
commitment of 1913 forced AT&T to divest itself of Western Union and to
stay out of telegraphy. The close relation of the two technologies brought the
phone company back in for one more foray in 1931 when it launched a
teletype service. In section 7.2.3 we described AT&T's acquisition of the
Teletype Corporation, the offering of TWX, and the eventual sale of it to
Western Union in the 1960s forced by government under anti-trust action. In
the last 15 years, with the development of computer networks, businesses

once more begun to use their phone lines to carry text between offices, and now value-added service vendors are offering this as a service over phone lines. The process now seems irreversable. The phone network has become the nation's teletype network too. Vail's hoped for merger of telegraphy and telephony into one utility company was indeed frustrated, but one of those is providing the network for the other.

8.1.9 Telephony leads to advances in sampling theory and statistics. (Type B)

Quality control was an important problem for a large system consisting of more or less independent franchised companies. In 1882 the new license contracts stipulated that

> At all times during their manufacture and upon their completion the instruments and the materials employed shall be subject to the inspection and acceptance . . . by said first party (American Bell Telephone Company).[24]

However, it was not until 1907 that the company attempted a rigorous, centralized quality control program. When that began, it required a scale of activities that could only be handled by sampling. As a result the Bell System became actively interested in sampling theory. Although the inspection function had been reorganized, its effect was minimal until more sophisticated and extensive quality control methods began to be developed in the mid-1920s.

The large telephone network had other statistical problems besides quality control. Before the turn of the century telephone companies became aware of marked diurnal rhythms in the use of the network, and of consequent peak-load problems.[25] Theoretical research into traffic control was undertaken by 1885 by G. T. Blood, E. C. Molina, and M. C. Rorty at the direction of Hammond Hayes. "The belief is common," wrote Rorty, "That, at the point where the human element enters a proposition, all recognized rules cease to hold."[26]

Hayes' group, however, rejected that notion. They believed in the utility of mathematical research into behavior, and their work eventually led to significant improvements in trunking and switching operations. In 1905 Hayes set up a separate Traffic Division under K. W. Waterson in the AT&T Engineering Department.

Note also that T. B. Doolittle, starting in 1893 or 1894, headed a division doing analysis of toll traffic as a basis for investment decisions.[27] Later statistical research extended to such subjects as word frequency counts in telephone conversations.[28]

8.1.10 Telephone system development stimulates research in city and regional planning.(Type B)

We have discussed in Section 2.1.7.2 the fact that about 1915 the telephone companies were the principle source of systematic demographic information on urban and neighborhood growth trends and characteristics. This data was collected partly by survey research methods; it contributed to the growth of a profession of planning.

8.1.11 Telephone system growth creates a need for advances in paper making and printing. (Type A)

Production of telephone directories presented mammoth printing problems. The volumes had to be cheap to permit free distribution. They had to be reprinted frequently because the system was growing rapidly, and because Americans are so geographically mobile.

Newsprint was the cheapest available paper, but the printing definition on it was poor, so fairly large type had to be used. To minimize the cost of phone books, it was desired to use the smallest legible type, but also cheap paper. To make that possible, telephone company researchers developed new types of low cost paper that would allow high definition with small type. They also made advances in printing technology including, for example, slugs that could be reused for the two-thirds of the entries that did not change between issues.[29]

Directories had to be printed and distributed quickly so as to be up-to-date. The operators' phone books around 1940 were revised every two weeks in New York City, every two days in Los Angeles, and daily in Detroit. The average production time from closing the text to delivery to subscribers was 35 days at that time. There were only five or six printing plants in the United States that could handle the job.[30]

8.2 The development of the telephone system as a stimulant to auxiliary businesses and services.

While the telephone is used in virtually every business, we shall here note a few of the services that are particularly reliant upon the telephone system for their operation.

8.2.1 Teleconferencing. (Type A)

In the United States, from a very early time, operators could and would set up connections among more than two parties.[31] On various occasions demonstrations were put on of the possibility of holding a meeting among a group of people in different locations. Articles were written suggesting that these would become increasingly popular. While conference call service is provided by AT&T, it has not become as popular or widely used as was sometimes anticipated.

Indeed, with the coming of electro-mechanical automatic switching the practicability of teleconferencing declined. It was not difficult for an operator to join several lines together. Automatic switches, however, were not built with that flexibility. In automatic systems the cost and difficulty of setting up conference calls is sufficiently great so that some systems, such as the Japanese system do not offer that service.

However, electronic switching is reversing that once more. A modern digital switch is a computer whose operations are governed by a stored program. In an SPC (stored program controlled) switch all sorts of complex operations can be added simply by modifying the software. The user can be provided with a set of input codes that will set up a multi-party call. Phone companies are, therefore, once more pushing conference calling as a new source of revenue—as fast as they move to digital switching. The computer switch will now do what the operator once did.

8.2.2 Information services. (Type A)

In the informal early days, the rural operator served as an information disseminator for anything of local interest. As systems grew and were formalized, rules came to govern what an operator was allowed to say. In different telephone systems specific information services were authorized. The most common ones were time and weather.[32] by the end of the 1930s, in the U.S., time was still being reported by live operators. The weather reports were already recorded. Dilts tells us that in New York City in the late 1930s the weather report was getting 20,000 calls a day, and time 60,000.[33] Today the figures are weather 145,000 a day, time 129,000.

Such services were readily introduced wherever, as in New York, there was metered local service, for they brought additional business to the phone company. In some places where there was unlimited local service, these calls were given an exchange number outside the unlimited zone; otherwise the phone company would have no incentive to offer them. Such a service can also be supported by advertising or by a voluntary group with a message it wants to promote.

In other countries more extensive information services have been offered, ranging from the full broadcasting program of the Budapest system described in section 4.7.1 on down. Paris and Shanghai, for example, offer shopping information. Sweden offered recorded reports on skiing, sailing, and swimming conditions.

Various companies offered theatre information. The Bengal Telephone Company in Calcutta had a general information bureau which offered such information to British subscribers as Hindustani words or the boiling point of water at different altitudes. Some U.S. rural phone companies offered various types of information for a while after the introduction of automatic dialing so as to reduce the trauma for their customers of the disappearance of the friendly operator.[34] However, since there was no way to collect revenue for such services, they tended to be abolished.

In most countries such information services declined as operators were eliminated, until the invention of recording on magnetic tape, after which such such services revived. The growth of recorded messages including those offered by private organizations, like dial-a-prayer, is a development that took place after the period of our study, for such messages depend upon electronic telephone answering equipment.

8.2.3 Call forward. (Type A)

Some systems offered a service allowing calls to be routed to another number when the receiving party was elsewhere, or providing for taking of messages by the operator if there was no answer. Shanghai provided that service. Call forward is now being introduced by AT&T in electronic exchanges, but such service has been handled in the past primarily by separate small telephone answering companies that grew up to supplement the system.

8.2.4 Recording and secretarial services. (Type A)

The Stockholm system would make a wax recording of a long distance conversation for a fee. The Paris company had secretaries on hand to take dictation over the phone, and had messenger boys who would pick up and deliver written matter for the customers. In the United States such services have been established, but are offered (along with answering services) by private companies, not the phone company itself. A Cleveland entrepreneur set up a telephone stenographic service in 1904, called a "Telagirl" system.[35]

8.2.5 Alarms. (Type A)

Burglar alarms, fire alarms, and storm warnings could be attached to the phone system either by the phone company itself or by other entrepreneurs. In Shanghai, for example, burglar alarm and typhoon warning services were offered by the phone company. In the section on emergency services (5.2.5, 5.2.6.1) we noted that various inventors and entrepreneurs developed alarms for use with the phone system.

8.2.6 Wake up. (Type A)

A morning call at a requested hour could be booked in many countries, for example Switzerland.

8.2.7 Taxi calling. (Type A)

In the U.S. today the usual system for getting a cab is a phone call to the taxi company, which in turn calls the cab by land-mobile radio. Before the days of land-mobile radio, and in countries where no such service is provided, the usual system is to have a phone in a street box at cab stands. The customer phones to a nearby cab stand.

8.2.8 Telephone marketing and polling. (Type A)

In sections 3.4.6 and 4.6 we described the use of the telephone in marketing and canvassing. Companies have been organized with a telephone bank in their premises to carry out such activities.

8.2.9 The telephone as a business "come-on." (Type A)

Before the general diffusion of coin telephones, and before the introduction of metered service, drug stores, cafes, and other merchants found it advantageous to allow potential customers to use the business' phone. By offering that favor they drew people in; alternatively, if a small charge were made the resulting revenue added to the merchant's income. The phone companies at first tried discouraging telephone moochers by writing in a clause against such activity in the contract and propagandizing against it in their ads. Needless to say, that was largely ineffective. The introduction of metered charges was a more effective stick against such generosity, and the introduction of coin phones with part of the revenue going to the premises was a more effective carrot.[36]

Hotels soon put telephones in every room. For one thing it cut the manpower needs for bellboys. Before the phone, the bellboy responded to a call bell, came upstairs to learn what was wanted, went down to fetch it, and came back again to deliver it. After the telephone he needed to make only the one trip, bringing what was requested; the first trip to learn the nature of the request was eliminated.[37] Furthermore, the hotel could levy a surcharge on calls that guests made. By 1904 the Waldorf Astoria logged over half a million calls a year on its 1120 phones.[38]

In 1912 Arnold Bennett wrote a series of articles in *Harper's Monthly* on a trip to the United States. One whole article dealt with the telephone as a pervasive feature of American society. He was astonished to discover a telephone in every hotel room. He was also shocked in a restaurant to have a telephone plugged in at his table. He predicted, "that on my next visit I shall find a telephone on every table of every restaurant that respects itself."[39] Bennett's prediction has proved wrong probably because the message charges on business phones and coin phone rate structure make the table phone economically unattractive to restauranteurs except in luxury restaurants.

The coin phone has remained a service for the convenience of customers, but the return is low enough so that increasingly, booths in the U.S. are put on the street rather than in stores.

8.3 The limitations of the phone system makes it the butt of humor and displaced aggressions. (Type B)

Particularly in the period of its' development, the telephone often worked less than perfectly. Thus users frequently expressed frustration at unintelligible sounds, squawks, and squeaks, crossed wires,[40] errors of recognition, late night phone calls, and wrong numbers. Sir William Thomson (later Lord Kelvin), commented enthusiastically on Bell's telephone at the Philadelphia exposition, but his remarks were largely devoted to noting which words were intelligible and which were not. The telephone, however, was then so novel that to produce anything intelligible was seen as a feat.[41]

Phone directories, in the early years, contained advice on speaking distinctly and directly into the mouthpiece.[42] Ambivalence about the phone was expressed from the beginning. On March 5, 1877, the New York Daily Telegraph ran a piece called "The Terrors of the Telephone." One of numerous satirical articles poking fun at the difficulty of telephone conversation was by Mark Twain in a Christmas piece in 1890. "Twain," writes Bruce,[43] "had as great a reverence as any American for technology in general, including the telephone, which as early as 1877 he had used as the basis for a short story of the science fiction genre." Nonetheless with a humorous cut in his 1890 piece in the *New York World*, he wrote; "It is my heart-warm and world-embracing Christmas hope and aspiration that all of us—the high, the low, the rich, the poor, the admired, the despised, the loved, the hated, the civilized, the savage—may eventually be gathered together in a heaven of everlasting rest and peace and bliss—except the inventor of the telephone." When Gardiner Hubbard, Bell's father-in-law, remonstrated with him, he replied in humor that he was a war with the Hartford phone company. No man, he said, could make a 20 word message intelligible over it in less than week. "And if you try to curse through the telephone they shut you off."

"Outrages of the Telephone" in *Lippincott's magazine*[44] substitutes moralism for Twain's humor. It complains about "talkative people wasting one's time."

An article in the *Bristol* (England) *Times* on November 7, 1879 complains that businessmen who have phones are interrupted by business calls during dinner.

The intrusiveness of the telephone (cf. section 10.6.6) is commented on further in a *Literary Digest* piece of 1912 on the "Telephone and the Doctor."[45] It likens the telephone to a long stethescope. "Its chief drawback is that, unlike the stethescope, it is not so easily taken out of the ears, and it brings him into communication with the world without when he would not, as well as when he would have it so." The following year the *Women's Home Companion*[46] discusses abuses of the telephone. One bereaved family had to have its phone disconnected because it could not make burial arrangements due to the sympathy calls. The previous month *American Homes and Gardens* had a piece on "telephone talk," also describing various annoyances and problems.[47]

In the 1920s a popular phonograph record was "Cohen on the Telephone".[48] It had an immigrant Jew with a strong accent struggling unsuccessfully to make himself understood on the telephone. An extreme version of the complaints about the telephone came from a Germany psychiatrist in 1912 who claimed that telephone nervousness is a serious disorder. At least one patient, he claims, was so worked up by delays and unpleasant experiences that he was rendered permanently insane. "Excitable persons," he says, "should never use the telephone."[49]

Another quaint objection to the phone was that of the National Conference of Old German Baptists, which ordered its members to stop using that "device of Satan," which makes people lazy, and for which "there is no warrant in Scripture."[50]

FOOTNOTES

[1]Clyde Jones in Evolution of the Telephone, in *Electrical Engineering,* 1893, noted the stimulus to scientific imagination represented by the telephone. Beyond the transmission of voice he anticipated video, and beyond that artificial eyes for the blind and "if life be but a manifestation of electrical energy" perhaps the secret of life (p.15).

[2]Dizard, *Business Planning and Telephone Research,* op. cit., p.24

[3]Ibid., p. 24.

[4]Bell Telephone Laboratories has done so in a multivolume series entitled *A History of Engineering and Science in the Bell System, vol. 1, The Early Years, 1875–1925: vol. 2, National Service in War and Peace, 1925–1975.* New York: The Laboratories 1975–1978.

[5]Cf. Waldon Fawcett. Successors of the Telephone. *Harper's,* Feb. 1902, *104,* 496.

[6]Dilts. *The Telephone in a Changing World,* p. 183.

[7]Cf. The Transmitophone. *Telephony,* Nov. 1906, *12* (5), 288–89; Church and Theatre Service By Telephone. *Telephony,* June 1907, *13* (6), 414.

[8]Jos. P. Maxfield, The Vitaphone—An Audible Motion Picture, *Bell Laboratories Record,* June 1926, pp. 200–204.

[9]Cf. sections 1.4.5.2 and 4.7.2.3.

[10]Cf. Major- General George O. Squire's The Unification of Communication   Engineering. *Scientific American,* Aug. 1922 *127,* 85, 142, 143. Also Wiley and Rice, *Communication Agencies and Social Life.*

[11]Bruce. *Bell* p. 242.

[12]Dilts. *The Telephone in a Changing World,* p. 22.

[13]Erik Barnouw. *A Tower in Babel: A History of Broadcasting in the United States*. New York: Oxford University Press 1966, p. 7.

[14]Fawcett. Successors of the Telephone, p. 497.

[15]E.M. Rotherie. Seeing Through the Telephone. *Telephony*, 2, Aug. *1906, 12* (2), 96.

[16]Rotherie. *Seeing Through the Telephone*, Epp. 96–97.

[17] The Universal Telephone. *Telephony*, Aug. 1906, *12* (2), 130.

[18]Casson. The Future of the Telephone pp. 12916–17.

[19]S.C. Gilfillan. The Future Home Theatre. *The Independent*. Oct. 17, 1912, *73*, 886–891.

[20]The Television Demonstration. *Bell Telephone Quarterly*, July 1927, *6* (3), 198.

[21]Notes on Recent Occurrences. *Bell Telephone Quarterly*, July 1930, *9* (3), 227.

[22]Herbert Ives. Picture Transmission and Television. *Bell Telephone Quarterly*, April 1932, *11* (2), 142.

[23]Federal Communications Commission, pp. 238–39.

[24]Dizard. *Business Planning and Telephone Research, 1875–1925*.

[25]Cf. Angus S. Hibbard. A Phase of Telephone Enginerering. *Electrical Engineering*, March 1894, *3* (3), 81–87.

[26]Dizard. *Business Planning and Telephone Research, 1875–1925*, p. 18

[27]Federal Communications Commission. *Investigation of the Telephone Industry in the United States, 1*, 88.

[28]Frequency of Words Used Over the Telephone. *Science*, Supplement August 14, 1931, *74*, 11–12.

[29]Dilts. *The Telephone in a Changing World*, pp. 136–141.

[30]Dilts. *The Telephone in a Changing World*, pp. 137–141.

[31]*Telephony* (April 1906, *11* (4), 243) in an article on "New Uses for Telephone" reported that the Billerica Board of Selectmen held a meeting by telephone during a storm; cf. Action At a Distance, p. 39.

[32]Cf. John D. Holland. Speaking Clock For Announcing Time To Subscribers. *Telephony* Dec. 30, 1911, *61* (27), 807–8. The device there reported used 72 wax cylinders, each with ten minutes of announcements, including ads. It was receiving almost 10,000 calls a day in Chicago. It was economical only with automatic switching.

[33]Dilts. *The Telephone in a Changing World*, pp. 126–128.

[34]Dilts. *The Telephone in a Changing World*, pp. 130f.

[35]The Telagirl System. *Telephony*, Aug. 1904:*8* (2); cf. Telephoning to a Phonograph. *Telephony*, p. 127, June 1905, *9* (6), 514.

[36]*Telephony*, in an article entitled "The Drug Store Pay Station Again," (Sept. 12, 1908, *16* (5), 218) said that New Orleans druggist, by agreeing all together to substitute coin boxes for free use of their phones "have got rid of the free telephone nuisance."

[37]An ad for hotel phone systems is quoted by Cherry ("The Telephone System," p. 119) from the *Melbourne Telegraph Electrical Society Journal* in the November-January, 1877–78 issue.

[38]Aronson. Bell's Electric Toy, p. 30.

[39]Arnold Bennett. Your United States, Fourth Paper.*Harper's* Bazaar, July 1912, *125*, 192.

[40]Cf. "Cross Wires," a poem by Arthur Crawford, *Harper's Bazaar*, Jan. 1913, *47*, 50, which mixes several telephone conversations.

[41]Dilts. *The Telephone in a Changing World*, p. 4.

[42]As late as 1913, the *Literary Digest* carried a description of an invention designed to improve the sound quality of a phone call by transmittion the vibrations in the nose. For an example of how to use the phone see Angus S. Hibbard. How to Use a Telehone, reprinted in Brosseau, *Looking Forward*, p. 81.

[43]Bruce. *Bell*, p. 285.

[44]Minna Thomas Antrim. Outrages of the Telephone. *Lippincott's Magazine*, July 1909, *84*, 126.

[45]The Telephone and the Doctor. *Literary Digest*, 44, May 18, 1912, *44*, 1037.

[46]A.S. Richardson. "Telephone Courtesy" *Woman's Home Companion*, March 1913, *40*, 43.

[47]Other articles expressing people's antipathies against the phone include: The Problem of the Telephone. *Scientific American*, Feb. 17, 1883: *48* (7), Back To the Land—And the Telephone. *The Spectator*, April 7, 1906, p. 530; Andrew Lang. The Telephone and Letter-Writing.*The Critic*, June 1906, *48*, 507–508; Telehone Manners. *Telephony*, Jan. 1907, *13* (1), 37; The Telephone. *Telephony*, no author June 8, 1910, *19* (2), 36; W.P., "P.S.: Telephonitis" Lippincott's Magazine, March 1913, *91*, 377–78.

[48]Mayer. The Telephone and Uses of Time, p. 240.

[49]Telephone a Cause of Insanity. *Telephony*, Oct. 19, 1912, *63*(16), 618.

[50]Samuel G. McMeer. Digest of Telephone Literature. *Telephony*, Aug. 1905, *10* (2), 134–35.

9

The Telephone and Social Structure

9.1 The telephone provides a bond for communities. (Type C)

9.1.1 The operator becomes a community agent. (Type A)

In the days before the multiple switchboard the relationship of operator and customers became such that customers often gave presents to the operator for her kindnesses.[1] The significance of the operator to her subscribers is a point already stressed repeatedly in various contexts. We have talked about the operator in rural life (section 2.2.1.6) and the operator and information services (section 8.2.2). These points need not be repeated.[2] Let us note only that when the operator disappeared a significant hole was left in many communities.

9.1.2 The telephone reduces loneliness. (Type C)

Probably no other assertion is made more frequently or documented less frequently. It seems to commentators obvious beyond the point of needing documentation. Two serious studies confirm the obvious, but both are well outside our period: one is Wurtzel and Turner's analysis of reactions to loss of phone service following a fire in a New York exchange.[3] The other is a study currently under way in Japan on the telephone in the life of women.[4] Fiction about the telephone also reflects this basic effect. As Brooks points out,[5] the lonely person clinging to the telephone in search of human contact is a repeated theme in song and story.

An interesting point made in *Recent Social Trends*, the report of the Commission set up by President Hoover, is the importance of the telephone directory in reducing social isolation.[6]

Particularly stressed in the literature on the telephone is the end of loneliness for the farmer and farmer's wife. (See section 2.2.1.1.)

9.1.3 The telephone increases social interactions. (Type C)

Numerous pieces by Mark Twain from 1878 on describe endless chatter on the telephone by housewives, adolescents, and indeed everyone.[7] The growth of "chat" is viewed by some positively and by others negatively. Bell viewed it

129

positively. He wrote to his wife Mabel when the phone was less than two years old; "When people can . . . chat comfortably with each other by telegraph over some bit of gossip, every person will desire to put money in our pockets by having telephones."[8] Others viewed idle telephone talk as a vice.

> A telephone in a residence should be for the convenience of the user, for imperative needs, for exceptional social emergencies, where writing, sending, or going is quite impossible—for sudden illness, for bad weather, for unavoidable delays, for trains, or service of any sort. For these things it is indispensable but for the exchange of twaddle between foolish women, communications between the prowling wolf and the unsuspecting lamb, it has become an unmitigated domestic curse.[9]

Other pieces note the broadening of the range of people who can talk to each other. "Telephone" is a poem by Joseph Hubbard that appeared in the *Atlantic Monthly*[10] which praises the instrument for its ability to put one in contact with anybody.[11]

9.1.4. The telephone produces communities without contiguity. (Type C)

That thesis was put forward by Suzanne Keller in the telephone centennial volume.[12] Other papers in that volume, notably Thorngren's[13] and to some degree Reid's[14] question it. The thesis is that for the first time communities can develop, thanks to the telephone, among people who do not live close to each other; they can form communities based on shared tastes and interests though they do not meet.

Here we do not ask how far this is true. It is a hypothesis. What is relevant to note here, however, is that (with one exception)[15] this hypothesis does not appear in clear form in the period before World War II. It is an anticipation that went beyond what people then were thinking about.

9.2 The telephone will provide a bond for family life. (Type B)

Occasionally in the 1930s one finds slight intimations of the reverse, particularly in sociological discussions. There is a tendency for social analysts to see some large sweeping trend in society and then to assume that all social forces work in that direction. One such broad trend that 20th century sociologists have repeatedly observed is the decline in the strength of family ties. Sometimes in writing about this an author would note the role of technological changes, noting the contribution to this trend of the automobile, the movies, contraceptives, etc. In such statements one sometimes finds the telephone mentioned in a list, but not discussed, for in fact if one examines it at all, it seems far more plausible that the telephone was a counter-force, providing a way of maintaining family ties.

Robinson, for example, in his *Improvement of Towns and Cities,* in 1901 noted the connection between telephone communication and family cohesion.[16] When a family moved to the suburbs the telephone was of critical importance, as we noted in section 5.1, for it meant that the wife at home was not totally cut off from her commuting husband in town. In case of emergency he had a way of reaching her. So too, young families as they moved out of the center city or to other communities could remain in some contact with their parents. Earlier, the migrant was forced to leave his relatives virtually once and for all; not so after the telephone.

9.3 The telephone will provide a window on the world for the elderly as they became less active outside. (Type C)

One human interest story we came across makes this point, at least implicitly. It describes a house-bound old lady on a party line who spent her time listening in on all her neighbors and butting into their lives.[17] The point was also made as early as 1879 in an article in *The Spectator* on "The Telephone Exchange."[18]

Nonetheless, this proposition does not show up often in our literature search of the period before World War II, though it is widely recognized now. A possible explanation is that old people are not early adopters of innovations. In a period when the telephone was new, perhaps its active users were younger people. We speculate; we do not know. Another possible explanation is that the telephone was expensive; old people could rarely afford it.

9.4 Women and the telephone.

We shall not here repeat the points made above about the telephone and loneliness (sections 2.2.1.1 and 9.1.2) or the telephone and security (sections 2.2.1.2 and 5.1), except to note that these considerations are often said to be particularly relevant to women. While men would be apt to be out at work, in the early years of the telephone the woman would often be at home alone with her small children.

Whether for that reason or others, one of the most common remarks about women and the telephone is to allege a peculiar addiction on their part to its use.

9.4.1 Women talk longer on the telephone than men. (Type D)

Apparently it is a fact, not just a sexist sterotype, that women's telephone conversations are longer than men's.[19] It certainly was the stereotype in fiction and essay ever since Mark Twain in 1880 wrote a sketch of a one-sided conversation of a woman on the phone.[20] The remarks are often savage like Twain's quote on "twaddle between foolish women,"[21] or friendlier but condescending like Arnold Bennett's:

There [in the U.S.] a woman takes to the telephone as women in more decadent lands take to morphia. You can see her at morn at her bedroom window, pouring confidences into her telephone, thus combining the joy of her innocent vice with the healthy freshness of breeze and sunshine.[22]

9.4.2 The use of women operators in manual exchanges significantly increases economic opportunities for women. (Type B)

Recently, the women's movement has altered employment patterns in the telephone business. AT&T's previous employment policy reserved operator's jobs for women, but allowed few women to reach executive rank. Today if one dials "O" one will often get a male voice. The lowered barriers represent progress for women today but at an earlier stage the reservation of jobs in a large and rapidly growing new occupation helped women to move into the big world.[23] At the turn of the century, if a young unmarried rural woman moved to the city, as millions did, her options were limited. Prevailing moral concepts made a sharp division between jobs in which she could retain her self-respect and those that forced her to work at a less desirable level. If she were educated she could be a teacher or nurse. If she had no special skills there were few options other than demeaning ones by the standard of the day, such as domestic service, waiting on table, or factory work. The opening up of jobs at telephone switchboards solved the problem for many young women. It was "one of the few trades in which woman workers are constantly . . . in demand."[24] It was work in an all female environment with no requirement to deal face-to-face with strange men. The phone company made the most of this attraction and featured the respectability of the job.[25]

The level of pay also reflected the values of the day and of the market. The phone company praised it as good pay for an unskilled, unmarried girl, while labor called it exploitation.[26] Objectively speaking, there were few other equally clean and respectable unskilled jobs at that time that paid much better,[27] though clearly by defining the job as one for a young unmarried girl the companies were keeping their costs down.

In any case burgeoning telephone employment in exchanges and on PBXs, like secretarial employment slightly later, offered a path to self-support and independence for millions of women. As early as 1907, for example, the telephone system employed 42,000 men and 50,000 women.[28]

9.5 The telephone and youth.

9.5.1 Young people will use the telephone more than their elders. (Type D)

The data on this piece of folklore is more mixed than that on women, but the stereotype of the adolescent hanging on the phone is well established in the U.S.[29] It is not necessarily true that present figures on telephone use by age, of which there are some,[30] applied to an earlier era when phones were a novelty and luxury. Yet adolescent chitchat on the phone appears in literature early, just as does women's chitchat. On the other hand, data from other countries, such as Japan, where all calls are metered, show less access to the phone by children and adolescents. Parents control calls that cost money. The system of unlimited local calling fosters the social use of the phone and its use by young people.

9.5.2 The phone will allow mothers to keep tabs on children. (Type A)

Leaving a phone number with the baby sitter or telling the child "phone me if you are going to stay there" or "let me know when you are coming home" is so familiar today that one wonders how mothers survived when there was no way to know where or how their offspring were.

We cannot say whether the ability of mothers to keep track implies greater or lesser freedom for the young. It might allow mothers to relax the limits on where the child may wander or it might result in more effective restraint on the child. What it clearly does do is to ease the mother's anxiety.

9.5.3 The telephone is a channel for safe sexuality. (Type D)

From early on some writers were shocked to discover young people using the phone for conversations of a kind in which they would not engage face to face. We previously noted a 1909 tirade against use of the phone for "communications between the prowling wolf and the unsuspecting lamb."[31] The same piece tells us that "impulsive women say things to men and to each other over the telephone that they would never say face to face." Four years later *Woman's Home Companion* comments "A young girl who would not think of standing on a street corner to converse with a boy will call him at his home by telephone and exchange idle nothings with him while members of his family pass comment on her lack of manners."[32]

The obscene caller is exercising an extreme version of seeking a vicarious thrill in safety; he seems not to appear in literature in the era before automatic dialing; there may not have been quite enough safety then.

In the Victorian era the sexual significance of the phone was evidenced by the large number of jokes about untoward happenings on the phone and by sentimental stories about telephone romances. *The New York Tribune's* story (Nov. 4, 1876) on the phone at the Philadelphia exposition could come up with only two prospective uses for this new device, of which one was for a lover to pop the question to a lady far away.[33]

FOOTNOTES

¹ Dilts. *The Telephone in a Changing World*, p. 107.

²But note also: Behind the Scenes at Central. *Booklover's Magazine*, Oct. 1903, *2*, 390–401; Sylvester Baxter. The Telephone Girl. *The Outlook*, May 26,   1906, *83*, 231–239.

³Cf. Wurtzel and Turner. Latent Functions of the Telephone, 246–260; section 5.1.

⁴Cf. Mayer. The Telephone and Uses of Time, p. 231.

⁵John Brooks. The First and Only Century of Telephone Literature. In Pool. *The Social Impact of the Telephone*. 213.

⁶President's Research Committee on Social Trends. *Recent Social Trends in the United States.*

⁷Mark Twain. A Telephone Conversation. Reprinted in Charles Neider (Ed.), *Complete Humorous Sketches and Tales of Mark Twain.* New York: Doubleday, 1961. Brooks. The First and Only Century of Telephone Literature.

⁸Quoted in Bruce, *Bell*, p. 210. Cf. Briggs. The Pleasure Telephone, for a discussion of the significance of "chat" and quotations about it.

⁹Antrim. "Outrages of the Telephone," *Lippincott's Magazine*, July 1909, p. 126.

¹⁰Joseph Hubbard. Telephone. *Atlantic Monthly*, Sept., 1914, *114*, 330–331.

¹¹Cf. Cherry. The Telephone System, p. 119, on democratizing of contacts.

¹²Suzanne Keller. The Telephone in New (and old) Communities. In Pool. *The Social Impact of the Telephone*, 293.

¹³Bertil Thorngren. Silent Action: Communication Networks for Development. In Pool. *The Social Impact of the Telephone*, 282–83.

¹⁴A.A.L. Reid. Comparing Telephone with Face-To-Face Contact. In Pool. *The Social Impact of the Telephone*, 346–411.

¹⁵Cf. Arthur Page's comment: "A man's neighbors are now more the people of his choice than those who happen to 'live next door.' " (Page. Social Aspects of Communication Development, p. 21.)

¹⁶Robinson. *Improvement of Towns and Cities.*

¹⁷Harriet Spofford. A Rural Telephone. *Harper's Monthly* May 1909, *118*, 830–837.

¹⁸The Telephone Exchange. *The Spectator*, Sept. 20, 1879, *52*, 1188.

¹⁹Mayer. The Telephone and Uses of Time, p. 231.

²⁰Mark Twain. A Telephone Conversation.

²¹Antrim, Outrages of the Telephone, *Lippincott's Magazine*, July 1909, 84, 126.

²²Bennett. Your United States, Fourth Paper, p. 192. Cf. Back to the Land— And the Telephone. *The Spectator*, April 7, 1906, p. 530; Page. Social Aspects of Communication Development, p. 23.

²³Brenda Maddox, Women and the Switchboard, In Pool. *The Social Impact of the Telephone.*

²⁴Good Points and Bad Points of Telephone Operating As a Trade for Philadelphia

²⁵There were also numerous stories on how good were the prospects of the operators for matrimony, and the implications of that for labor turnover. Men were reportedly con-

[25]There were also numerous stories on how good were the prospects of the operators for matrimony, and the implications of that for labour turnover. Men were reportedly constantly falling in love with the unseen voice. Cf. Cupid Cripples Muncie "Central". *Telephony*, Aug. 1904, *8*, (2), 123.

[26]Anne Withington. When the Telephone Girls Organized. *The Survey*, Aug. 16, 1913, *30*, 621–23.

[27]Cf. Switchboard Positions in Demand. *Telephony*, Nov. 1905, *10* (5), 363.

[28]Mumford. This Land Of Opportunity. The Industry's perspective is given in an article—Telephone Operators Hard To Get. *Telephony*, June 1905, *9* (6), 485—which discusses the increasing difficulty in securing and retaining the right kind of female labor. It discusses incentives, training schools, and perceptions of the relative merits of different ethnic groups. Morale building paeans to "The Telephone Girl" were also common. Cf. Sylvester Baxter. Telephone Girl. *The Outlook*, May 26, 1906, *83*, 231–39, also *Telephony*, Jan. 1907, *13* (1) 37.

[29]See McLuhan. *Understanding Media*, p. 233.

[30]See Mayer. The Telephone and Uses of Time, pp. 229ff.

[31]Antrim, "Outrages of the Telephone" p. 126.

[32]A. S. Richardson Telephone Courtesy. *Women's Home Companion*, March, 1913, *40*, 43.

[33]It added "it is not for us to guess how courtships will be carried on in the Twentieth Century." Other romantic discussions of the telephone include: Heard on the Party Line. *Telephony*, July 1904, *8* (1), 75; Long Distance Telephone Weddings. *Telephony*, Aug. 1904, *8* (2), 117; The Secret Service. *Telephony*, June 1907, *13* (6), 415 on the advantages for lovers of dial phones without operators. *The Spectator*, April 7, 1906, suggested "that a new method of rustic courtship may be added to the three stages already existing"—walking-out, courting, and being engaged—namely "talking."

10

Social Customs and Practices

10.1 Telephoning for appointments will become customary. (Type A)

In writings about the tradeoff between visiting people in person and phoning, it is often forgotten that one of the main uses of the telephone is to arrange appointments. Almost every visit today requires at least one phone call first.

In the days before the telephone, custom allowed one to visit unannounced to pay one's respects; at certain times the house had to be prepared for such guests. If no one was home, or if the residents hid upstairs, the caller would leave a card. That kind of visiting was effectively ended by the telephone.

For other more formal occasions it had been customary to send written invitations to which a written reply was expected. Various observers noted and some deplored the tendency to substitute a phone call.[1] Hendrick noted that in 1914 White House wedding invitations were by phone.[2] The previous year, Anna Seese Richardson in the *Woman's Home Companion* complained about the impoliteness of a phoned acceptance of an invitation and warned that phoned invitations taken as messages may not get delivered, or if not noted down may be forgotten.[3]

10.2 Codes of telephone courtesy will develop. (Type B)

Etiquette books and articles advised on how to answer the phone.[4] Normal conduct did not always correspond to the advice being given. For example, people were repeatedly exhorted not to say "hello" but to identify themselves, for instance, "Mrs. Smith calling."[5] They rarely did.[6]

Profanity was one topic harped upon in discussions of telephone manners.[7] A female operator on the line was considered to require callers to avoid bad language. Phone companies sometimes cut off service to those who swore. It will be recalled that one of Mark Twain's complaints was against the Hartford company's efforts to control his language. In 1904 a Paris journalist was fined for using strong language to the "demoiselle de telephone." He refused to pay; the police seized his furniture and the case because a *cause celebre* in the Chamber of Deputies.[8]

10.3 Telephone manners will tend toward informality. (Type B)

The decline of written invitations, the willingness of people to say things they would not say face to face, the ambiguous greeting "hello" before the speaker is identified, the fact that anyone may answer the call, master or servant, male or female, young or old, all tended in the direction of breaking down some of the older formal conventions of social interaction. Mrs. C. S. Peel,[9] reviewing social life before World War I, wrote that the "telephone has helped . . . make life less formal."

10.4 Conventional styles will develop for telephone conversation. (Type B)

Serious analysis of the linguistic or structural patterns of telephone conversation do not appear early. The styles of conversation, however, in various literary passages, give testimony to the presence in early telephone practice of forms which have been analyzed more recently.[10] Thus phone conversations generally begin by the receiver of the call saying "hello" upon picking up the phone.[11] The caller then replies "hello" and adds any one of several phrases which Schegloff has analyzed and categorized. These include such items as "How are you?" or "Is John in?" The striking point is that in calls among friends, both parties are reluctant to identify themselves first; the caller tries to lead the receiver to recognize the caller by voice and context. When the receiver has recognized the caller, the response is generally "hello, Mary" or whatever the caller's name may be. A psychological theory of this caution about self-identification in the absence of sight has not yet been offered, nor have these American findings been examined cross-culturally.

There are also conventions for situations like wrong numbers. Most people expect the caller to state the number he wanted to reach ("Is this 458-9921?") rather than for the receiver to state the number reached. To reveal the number reached is believed to provide some valuable information to a malevolent caller, although presumably he already knows well the number he dialed. So the convention arises more from psychological guardedness than from any rational analysis of risks.

There are also conventions for terminating telephone conversations. Most people feel that they have been rude if they take the lead in closing a call that they received. That should by done by the caller.

10.5 The quality of letter writing will decline. (Type C)[12]

Anna Richardson comments in 1913 that "In a household where the telephone habit has gripped the rising generation it is not unusual to hear the daughter beg their mothers or aunts, or even grandmothers, to help them compose a simple note of congratulation or condolence."[13] The decline in writing skill was a common complaint.[14]

10.6 The telephone increases and decreases privacy.
(Type C)

As we noted in the introduction, we do not know which way the net effect of the telephone went; in some ways it increased privacy, in other ways it decreased it;[15] its net impact is unclear.

Concern about privacy has been present all through the century, though it tended to be subdued in discussing problems where it seemed nothing could be done about it, and more active when ways of protecting it became apparent. For example, the issue of privacy loomed large in the earliest days of wireless telegraphy, since people then realized that there was a choice between sending messages over a wired rather than a wireless system. In 1899 J. A. Fleming, a wireless pioneer, published an article on the "scientific History and future Uses of Wirless Telegraphy" in *North American Review*.[16] He concluded that wireless "will never replace entirely telegraphy with wires, because the use of the continuous wire secures a privacy not otherwise to be obtained."

Yet when over-the-air transmissions came to be used for ship communications right after the turn of the century, for police car communications twenty years later, for transatlantic phone calls in 1927, for microwave long-lines circuits since World War II, and for satellite communications now, it has been only under the most extreme circumstances that users have worried about invasion of their privacy or tried to do anything about it. Some sensitive business transactions are coded. For the last few years the federal government has put its domestic national security traffic on cable rather than on microwave circuits, because it established that the Soviet Embassy was listening in. But on the whole the revealed consumer preference for spending money on privacy is rather small. Most people will not spend much to reduce the risk that someone is listening to them.

Indeed, the behavior of people in phone booths or on the street shows an unparanoid assumption that the people passing by who can certainly overhear their words, are neither paying attention nor trying to listen in. The simple and effective Hush-a-Phone type of device that surrounds the mouthpiece with a muffler has not taken hold.

So if telephonic invasions of privacy have occurred (as they have), it is at least in large part because users chose not to do what they could have done—at a cost—to protect themselves. Nonethelss, when violations of the public's basic trustfulness have been exposed in bugging scandals, the American public has turned indignant,[17] and of course some individuals of a secretive temperament have been suspicious of surveillance all the time.

The real effect of the telephone on privacy has not been that of the phone as an abstract concept, but that of the phone system as it was actually built, with its various protections and lacks of more protections. The net effect on privacy probably did not deviate very far from what people were used to, for if it had there was plenty of opportunity to enhance the security of the system, or conversely to save money by reducing security. So the system could always move to a preferred equilibrium.

The ways in which the phone system both increased and decreased privacy were not inevitable but were features of the system as it worked in practice.

10.6.1 Party-Line phones require people to converse in the hearing of others. (Type E)

For many years party-line listening-in was a basic feature of rural life repeatedly joked about or treated in fiction.[18] The very first known telephone ad issued by Gardner Hubbard in May 1877 pointed out that "the use of more than two phones on the same line where privacy is required is not advised."[19] Inventions were made and promoted to prevent party-line listeners, for instance to signal the callers when a third receiver was raised.[20]

These issues, of course, vanished as open party lines disappeared.

10.6.2 Operator attended calls can be heard by the operator. (Type B)

This kind of possible scrutiny of one's conversations passed with automatic dialing.[21] Pending that, various states passed laws prohibiting phone company employees from revealing what they heard.[22] These laws followed a well established precedent of laws sealing the lips of telegraphers.

10.6.3 Concern about telephone tapping will rise if the likelihood of actual listeners-in declines. (Type B)

No great outpouring of indignation about telephone tapping occurred in the days when operators could listen in if they had any reason to, and in which neighbors too could listen in on party-lines.[23] Dilts, for example, as late as 1941, wrote in praise of the FBI that it "knows the science of wiretapping thoroughly." She adds that "When calls are made between high ranking officers of our State Department and the heads of other governments the full force of surveillance is always in play."[24] At that time such practice seemed normal enough and not something to be mentioned only in criticism. Earlier, the Supreme Court in the case of Olmstead et. al. v. U.S. (48 Sup. Cf. 564, 1928) rejected the defendants' attempt to have evidence collected by a tap thrown out as in violation of the Fourth Amendment on searches and seizures and the Fifth Amendment on compulsory self-incrimination. Chief Justice Taft, in a decision that has since been overturned, ruled that there was no compulsion; the defendants were "voluntarily transacting business without knowledge of the interception." As to the Fourth Amendment he said that unlike the opening of sealed letters, "there was no searching. There was no seizure. The evidence was secured by the use of the sense of hearing, and that only."

Yet wiretapping was a matter of some concern even then. Brandeis and Butler wrote dissents to Olmstead. In his dissent Brandeis pointed out that 25 states had enacted statutes since 1912 prohibiting the interception of messages sent by telephone and/or telegraph, and that 35 states, starting in 1910, had made it a criminal offense for telephone and/or telegraph companies or their employees to disclose the content of messages.[25]

Concern about governmental wiretapping, however, grew in the era of automatic dialing, at which time people tended to assume that their conversations could be, and therefore should be, impervious to listeners-in. In 1944 the *Bell Telephone Laboratories Record* noted a growing concern over governmental recordings of conversations. In the 1960s and 1970s, this concern became a major public issue. There is far more concern than ever before about "big brother" watching each of us.

10.6.4 Every individual will be given a unique ID number to facilitate telephone service. (Type A)

In 1910 Casson[26] reports (without alarm or shock) that the phone company is working on a scheme to give each person a unique ID number, which would make it possible to phone to a person, wherever he happened to be located at that moment, instead of phoning to a number representing nothing more than a handset in a fixed location; the person we want to talk to might or might not happen to be there.

Something like the scheme that Casson described, which was quite impractical with electro-mechanical automatic switches, is now becoming possible with electronic Stored Program Controlled (SPC) switches. Many subscribers on SPC exchanges have opted for "call forward" service which allows them, when they are not at their usual number, to specify the number where they will be and to have the call transferred there. That still does not require a number for the individual, but only for each phone. However, it is a practical software modification to allow an individual like a travelling salesman to subscribe to a personal number and then to notify the SPC common-control system of the phone number he is at each time he moves. His office or other caller could then call him by entering his personal number and the system would find him, wherever he might be.

That is, of course, a purely voluntary system to which the customer chooses to subscribe and therefore quite different from a universal compulsory ID.

A required ID Number for each individual is the nightmare of contemporary civil libertarians and has long since been dropped from phone company planning. It would arouse too much fear that the number might become a universal ID used for all sorts of tracking, as indeed the phone number has sometimes become for family units.

10.6.5 Phone numbers will be used for identification and credit checking. (Type A)

This is not a development that we find anticipated in writings from before World War II. Yet it has happened. By now to open a charge account, get a credit card, or even cash a check, one must usually provide one's phone number. Use of phone numbers for such purposes would not have been nearly as feasible in the days before telephone penetration became virtually universal.

10.6.6 The telephone will be highly intrusive into domestic peace. (Type C)

Very few people can let the phone ring without answering it. From Mark Twain on,[27] people have commented on the imperious character of the phone bell, or upon the difficulty of hanging up.[28] The caller has no way of knowing what he is interrupting. The receiver no way of knowing who is calling or why. That too may change in future digital networks with common control signalling, for the information on the calling number can be retained and displayed on a screen at the receiving phone. But that is for the future. Until now the telephone's ring has remained an imperious command from one knows not whom.

Rice and Willey commented in 1933 that "personal isolation—inaccessibility to the demands of others for access to one's attention—is increasingly rare, or, when desired, increasingly difficult to achieve." They tabulated the average interval between incoming messages received by the average individual through different media in 1907 and 1927, and discovered that the telephone "is by far the most intrusive of the several agencies," and increasingly so.[29]

On the other hand, as we noted in section 10.1, the phone has decreased the incidence of unannounced visits. It is hard to balance the usually brief and in any case less upsetting requirement to handle phone calls against the rarer but more involving event of a surprise visit.

10.6.7 The telephone permits communications about sensitive matters without commitment to writing. (Type A)

The decline of written records was noted previously in section 4.2.3; the decline in letter writing skill was discussed in section 10.5, and in the next chapter we will note the consequence for historians (section 11.3.2). Here we discuss the decline in written communication in relation to its special consequence of helping avoid the creation of potentially embarrassing written records.

H. G. Wells noted this in 1902. "The businessman may sit at home . . . and tell such lies as he dare not write."[30]

Thus in some respects the phone has promoted privacy while undermining it in others, and it has done each to different degrees at different stages of the development of the technology.

FOOTNOTES

¹ Cf. W.P. "P.S.: Telephonitis" *Lippincott's Magazine*, 1913, *19*, 337.

² Hendricks. Telephones for the Millions.

³ Anna Steese Richardson. Telephone Courtesy. *Woman's Home Companion*, March 1913, *40*, 43.

⁴ Etiquette on the Telephone. *Telephony*, Sept. 1906, *12* (3), 186–7.

⁵ Bad Telephone Manners. *Telephony*, Aug. 1904, *8* (2), 130; Telephone Courtesy. *Telephony*, July 1904, *8* (1), 32.

⁶ Telephone Good Form. *Telephony*, Sept. 1907, *14*(3), 138.

7 Bad Telephone Manners. *Telephony*, Aug. 1904, *8* (2), 130.

⁸ Telephone Agitation in Paris. *Telephony*, Aug. 1904, *8* (2), 135.

⁹ C.S. Peel. *A Hundred Wonderful Years: Social and Domestic Life of a century, 1820–1920.* New York: Dodd, Mead, 1927, p. 8, quoted in Perry. The British Experience, 1876 – 1912. Cf. Richardson. Telephone Courtesy; Telephone Good Form. *Telephony*, Sept. 1907, *14* (3), p. 138.

¹⁰ For a recent examination of telephone style see Schegloff.Identification and Recognitions in Interactional Openings. In Pool. *The Social Impact of the Telephone.*

¹¹ Telephone Good Form. *Telephony*, Sept. 1907, *14* (3), 138.

12 Cf. Section 4.2.3 and 11.3.

¹³ Richardson. Telephone Courtesy.

¹⁴ Cf. Andrew Lang. Telephones and Letter Writing. *The Critic*, June 1906, *48*, 507–508.

¹⁵ Cf. Ogburn. *Technology and International Relations*, pp. 282.

¹⁶ J.A. Flemming. May 1899, 168, 630–40. Scientific History and Future Uses of Wireless Telegraphy. *North American Review.*

¹⁷ In other democratic countries such as France and Italy the public's reaction to government bugging seems to be more fatalistic. And in non-democratic countries it is of course assumed, even if resented.

¹⁸ Cf. Dalton Trumbo. *Johnny Got His Gun.* New York: Monogram Publishers, 1939. Brooks, "The First and Only Century of Telephone Literature."

¹⁹ Reproduced in *Telephony*, July 1904, *8* (1), 65.

²⁰ Baird Secret-Service Telephone. *Telephony*, Aug. 1905, *10* (2), 179; More Trouble For Telephone Listeners. *Literary Digest*, Nov. 21, 1914, p. 1005; Frank G. Moorhead, To Stop Telephone Eavesdropping. *Literary Digest*, Oct. 17, 1914, p. 733; Improving Telephone Service. *American Architecture*, Dec. 18, 1918, *114*, 753.

²¹ Also, devices were invented to prevent operators listening. Cf. L.W. Stanton. The Telephone System of the Future. *Scientific American Supplement*, May 19, 1906, *61*, 25, 399.

²² Eavesdropping Must Stop on Telephone Lines in Ohio. *Telephony*, April 10, 1909, *17* (15), 446. Cf. section 10.6.3.

²³ But see Lang. Telephones and Letter Writing.

²⁴ Dilts. *The Telephone in a Changing World*, pp. 83ff.

²⁵ In addition the series of devices that we noted earlier to provide privacy on party lines and against eavesdropping or tapping. Cf. Fawcett Waldron, How Uncle Sam Uses the Telephone. *Telephony*, Jan. 22, 1910, *19* (4), 90; Secret Telephone. *Scientific American*, Dec. 5, 1919, *121*, 555, on scrambling.

[26] Casson. Future of the Telephone, pp. 12903ff.

[27] Cf. section 8.3; McLuhan. *Understanding Media,* p. 235.

[28] Richardson. Telephone Courtesy, p. 43.

[29] See p. 93, fn. 58, Willey and Rice, *Communication Agencies and Social Life,* p.152. The telephone call receipt rate per person was one call every 3 days in 1907, one every 1-1/2 days in 1927. Letters came next in february.

[30] Wells. *Anticipations,* p.66.

11

The Telephone in Relation to Learning and Culture

11.1 The Telephone and Science and Technology.

Section 8.1 of this report was devoted to telephone related research and development and its results in producing technological progress. Some of the topics we discussed there, such as the development of statistical or city planning methods, could also fall under this topic.

The order of treatment is arbitrary, and we shall not repeat those points again. Some additional points have been made by various authors about the telephone's contribution to science and technology through learning and culture rather than through specific telephone research and development activities.

11.1.1 The telephone system will create employment openings for the college trained. (Type C)

That was a fairly central point in John Kimberly Mumford's 1908 article on the telephone, entitled "This Land of Opportunity".[1] He stresses the complexity and sophistication of the system and its dependence on high quality management. And so, Mumford reports, AT&T had begun systematic recruitment of college graduates. Mumford attributes the increased evaluation of a college education not to the phone company alone, but to the management needs of large corporations in general. He quotes Carty:

> The corporations are standing at the doors of the colleges with their hats in their hands . . . It's the trusts that have brought this condition about. It was no longer a question whether the graduate could get a job or not. The question was which job he would condescend to take.[2]

The telephone opportunities were greatest for those graduates with technical training. Said Carty:

> The Western Electric Company . . . was first to recognize the utility of college men as recruits in the engineering field. It began as far back as

145

1875 [before the phone!] to take a few of the best men from graduating classes and put them to work at $10 a week.[3]

11.1.2 The telephone system contributes to the establishment of the profession of electrical engineering. (Type C)

Electric power and telegraphy were developing at the same time as telephony; radio developed shortly thereafter. Among them they created what is now one of the larger professions. In 1882 MIT started teaching electrical engineering and by 1884 the first such departments were established at Cornell University and at Stevens Institute of Technology.

11.1.3 The telephone will stimulate interest in science. (Type C)

The latter part of the 19th century was a period of wide lay enthusiasm for science. Public lectures on science attracted large audiences. In London, the Royal Institution drew from the cream of the society for its Friday lectures. Graham Bell turned to giving public lectures on the telephone as a way of supporting himself and his work in the first couple of years after his invention. There was a wide popular interest in the miracle of the phone and how it worked.

As the phone became an everyday fact of life, particularly after 1915, lay publications about the phone, interest in it, and indeed understanding of it declined. That, however, was not what the earlier commentators predicted. They expected an ever growing interest and enthusiasm as the phone became more pervasive. Indeed, Casson in 1910 predicted that one of the social consequences of the phone would be a growing popular understanding of the scientific principles on which it works.[4]

11.2 The telephone will facilitate dissemination of knowledge. (Type A)

Among those early commentators who foresaw the telephone being used as a broadcasting mass medium, many expected it to be a powerful force for the dissemination of education and culture. S. C. Gilfillan's 1912 forecast of video courses carried by phone lines is one of the fuller descriptions.[5]

The expectation of broadcasting by telephone has, of course, not materialized. The telephone is used on a small scale for education of shut-ins and for remote schools.[6] It is also very actively used in the mass media as noted in section 4.7.2. Computer networks are a new and very important use of the telephone which could not be anticipated in the period we are studying. Beyond that the role of the telephone in scientific and educational institutions has been significant in more or less the same ways as in other large institutions, rather than in the ways anticipated.

11.3 The telephone will reduce emphasis on writing and increase emphasis on oral communication. (Type C)

11.3.1 The telephone will lower emphasis on writing skills in the schools. (Type C)

In sections 10.5 and 4.2.3 we noted a decline in the quality as well as quantity of letter writing both in institutions and in personal life. A decline of skills in handwriting and other writing skills has also often been noted. Attribution of the decline in letter writing to the telephone was common, but we do not find explicit discussions of how that decline in letter writing affected emphasis on writing in the schools. This forecast of a change in educational priorities was apparently not made on the record.

11.3.2 The decline in letter writing reduces the record available to historians. (Type C)

This forecast, often put forwad in recent years, was apparent on the record only late in the period we are studying. In 1935 Hector Bolitho wrote an article on "the Telephone and the Biographer"[7] in which he deplores the effect of the phone in making detailed reconstruction of a famous person's life or of negotiations almost impossible. In general, most early analyses tended to carry inferences only one step. They saw a decline of letter writing resulting from the use of the telephone. They rarely asked the next question, what a decline in letter writing would do in turn.

11.3.3 Writers of fiction and drama will use the telephone as a symbol and as a mechanism for moving the dramatic action. (Type D)

This proposition too was not seriously discussed until recently, though the frequent appearance of the telephone in song and story was recognized. The nature of this coverage has been analyzed by Brooks.[8] He finds that the telephone appears more in the period before World War II, when it was novel than recently when it is taken for granted.[9] In the earlier period the phone sometimes symbolizes the eerie and the supernatural.[10] Often the phone is used in plays to overcome the locational limits of a stage. Monologue into a telephone (like Twain's 1880 piece) was a new device for the writer, and one that required virtuosity in capturing a novel style of language.

11.3.4 The style of telephone conversation will modify the language. (Type C)

General Carty asserted in 1891 that telephone and telegraph had affected the use of language, creating a "telegraphic brevity," and he expected the use of recordings instead of written letters to improve elocution.[11] In 1905 *Telephony* predicted that in 50 years the phone system of numeration would be in use throughout. For example the number 2,884,377 would be read in the same manner as one would read a phone number: "number two double eight, four, three, double seven."

> Teacher—Johnny, what is the product of one double two nine by eight double seven?
>
> John (after due time)—one, O, double seven, double three.[12]

Telephony frequently made reference to the emerging changes in the use of language.

> That the telephone is giving the American voice a tone of culture and refinement, is the assertion of students who have investigated the subject. The result which generations of "finishing schools" have been trying to accomplish has been secured for young women in a few years by the telephone.[13]

The reader may recall that in section 4.1.1 on the disappearance of dialects we quoted Edward J. Hall, president of the Southern Bell Telephone and Telegraph Company, as saying there will be no dialects—no southern, no northern, no western accent—but instead just "one harmonious American language."[14]

Telephony in the same issue suggested "that a constant use of the telephone may improve enunciation and produce a sharp, clear cut conversational tone" among operators and others who talk on the phone continually, but "that its use can bring about any such desirable reformation in the man who talks into it perhaps a dozen or twenty times a day for three or four minute periods is not very probable." The following year, however, it quoted the head of the Voice Department of the Emerson College of Oratory in Hopkinsville, Kentucky predicting that because of the telephone the next generation or two would develop clear, precise enunciation[15] Dr. Frank H. Vizetelly, editor of *The New Standard Dictionary*, is quoted in the *Bell Telephone Quarterly* in 1930 as expressing "the great debt we owe these (telephone) companies for their efforts on behalf of standardized speech."[16]

In these comments from trade journals the emphasis is on the good things telephony may do for oral speech, rather than on any deleterious effects on formal or written speech, but in any case there is recognition of an impact.

FOOTNOTES

[1] John Kimberly Mumford. This Land of Opportunity, The Nerve-Center of Modern Busines, *Harper's Weekly*, Aug. 1, 1908, 52, 22–24.

[2] Ibid, p. 23.

[3] Mumford. This Land of Opportunity, p. 23.

[4] Casson. The Future of the Telephone.

[5] Cf. section 8.1.7; Gilfillan. The Future Home Theatre.

[6] Education By Telephone. *Telephony*, 1904, *8*, 25. Cf. Paladugu V. Rao. Telephone and Instructional Communications. In Pool. *The Social Impact of the Telephone*.

[7] Hector Bolitho. The Telephone And the Biographer. *The Spectator*, July 19, 1935, *155*, 90–97.

[8] Brooks. The First and Only Century of Telephone Literature.

[9] In its early years *Telephony* would run a short story about the telephone every few isues. It also ran numerous human interest anecdotes, usually turning on the peculiarities of telephone conversation. Cf. *Telephony*, Dec. 1902, *2* (6), 268f; Aug. 1904, *8* (2), 130.

[10] It will be recalled that Mark Twain wrote a science fiction story based on the phone as early as 1877.

11 The Prophet's Corner, *Electrical Review*, Aug. 29, 1891, *19* (1), 2.

[12] Numeration by the New Plan. *Telephony*, July, 1905, *10* (1), 77.

[13] Telephone Makes the Voice Soft. *Telephony*, Nov. 1905, *10* (5), 360.

[14] The Telephone Voice. *Telephony*, June, 1906, *11* (6), p. 382, quoted in Section 4.1.1.

[15] *Telephony*, Jan. 1907, *13* (1), 13.

[16] W.P. Banning. Better Speech. *Bell Telephone Quarterly*. April 1930, *19* (2), 80.

12

Conceptions of Self and Universe

We close with the most abstruse effects of the telephone and the hardest to identify, namely its effects, if any, on peoples' thoughts. Does the ability to conquer distance give people a sense of power? Does it generate hubris about human ability to conquer nature? Does it, as Erwin Canham suggests, give "man the attributes traditionally assigned to the deities: omnipresence, omniscience, omnipotence."[1]Such questions are much harder to answer than the ones with which we have dealt so far. Up to now we have traced the impact of a tangible physical device the telephone. One can observe how people use it, when they call, when they do not, whom they seek to reach, and how much time and money they spend on it. Those are empirical facts. Now we turn to a different kind of question, a question about the impact on people's thoughts of the Platonic image of the phone which they had in their minds. That is far harder to fathom.

Yet some such propositions about the telephone and conceptions of self and universe did appear in the literature.

12.1 The telephone will foster sociability and cooperativeness. (Type C)

These are the words of Herbert Casson; in 1911 he said the telephone "has enabled us to be more social and cooperative. It has literally abolished the isolation of the separate family."[2]

12.2 The telephone will foster impersonality. (Type C)

The introduction of phone numbers[3] led to some resentment of the impersonality of telephone relations. There were articles on how to remember telephone numbers.[4]There were also numerous comments on the inadequacies of contacts in which smiles and expressions could not be seen.

12.3 The telephone will change people's sense of distance. (Type C)

This point is but a corollary of the various points made about the ability of the telephone to conquer distance (Cf.sections 1.3., 2.1.6, 3.1.1, 4.9). Presumably these points may have profound psychological aspects too. Do people who have grown up from childhood talking to relatives long-distance across a continent have the same sense of distance as their ancestors a hundred years ago? We do not know; there is no solid evidence.

12.4 Religious and occult beliefs will have to take account of the telephone. (Type D)

Although religion was not a frequently mentioned topic it did appear on occasion. As discussed previously (section 8.3), the National Conference of Old German Baptists had adopted a resolution ordering all members of the church to discontinue the use of telephones. They argued that the telephone is a device of Satan, that it makes people lazy, and that there is no warrant in Scripture for its use.

On the opposite side the Chicago Christian Endeavor Union announced its plans to save 100,000 souls within one year by calling lists of unconverted friends of members.[5] The evangelists' contemporary leadership in using satellite/cable networks or the Ayatollah Khomeni of Iran's leadership in using international phone calls from Paris recorded on cassette tape recorders in Teheran to promote his revolution against the Shah is part of a long tradition. Those who are convinced that they know the truths that others should believe, can be quite innovative in accepting new means for achieving their mission.

A 1909 issue of *Telephony* cited a Los Angeles report that the telephone companies in the area had noted a material increase in use of their lines following the use of the telephone for "absent treatment" of patients by Christian Scientist healers.

12.5 The telephone system will create a spirit of service. (Type C)

"Service" was one of the key slogans of the Bell System. The company publicized heroism by operators and linesmen. Such stories appeared frequently in the general press.[6] Probably, however, that spirit owes more to the perspective that Vail brought to the company, than to anything inherent in the telephone. Coming from the public service, Vail saw the building of a telephone system as not only a business but a mission. It was this resolution to service over immediate profits that caused his retirement from the company from 1887 to 1907.

A different theory of this altruistic spirit is found in an interesting article by Frederic A. C. Perrine, in *Electrical Engineering,* in 1894.[7] He noted a marked difference between electrical engineers and other engineers in the spirit of social reform. Anyone prominent in electrical invention is likely in some period of his life to have "bent his energies toward some phase of reforming political economy." He notes the prominence in the first electrical congress in Paris of former St. Simonians. He attributes this confluence to the unlimited horizons of electrical science.

12.6 Beyond telephony lies telepathy and psychic powers. (Type B)

A few of the more starry-eyed writers on the telephone saw it as but a stage toward man's ability to communicate by means as yet unknown, perhaps from brain to brain.[8] In a slightly less specific vein various writers at the turn of the century predicted that within the 20th century a new means of transmitting intelligence would be found superceding all the physical barriers on telephony and telegraphy.[9] Sometimes these far-flung fantasies were camouflaged in jest; like all jokes they nonetheless conveyed someone's thoughts.[10]

FOOTNOTES

[1] Erwin Canham. *Awakening: The World at Mid-Century.* New York: Longman's Green, 1950, p. 8.

[2] Casson. The Social Value of the Telephone.

[3] Initiated in 1879 in Lowell, Mass. during a measles epedemic to reduce dependency on experienced operators, in case they became ill. AT&T *Events in Telephone History,* PE-109, AT&T, Sept. 1974.

[4] E.g., A Mental Telephone Index. *Atlantic Monthly,* July 1912, *110*, 140–42.

[5] A number of experiments were made in offering church services by telephone. Cf., Church Services By Telephone. *Telephony,* July 1904, *8* (2), 35; Church and Theatre Service By Telephone. *Telephony,* June 1907, *13* (6), 414–15.

[6] Cf. Enos A. Mills. Linemen Heroes on the Crest of the Continent, p. 14; Allen Tupper True. The Trouble Hunter. *Scribner's Magazine,* Jan. 1911, *49*, 92–102; The Linemen's Devotion to His Job. *Literary Digest,* March 14, 1/8914, *48, 572ff.*

[7] Perrine. *Electrical Engineering and Social Reform.*

[8] Cf. *Electrical Engineering,* "Comment and Clippings" 1893, *2*, 347.

[9] Cf. Harry S. Coyle. Evolution of Intelligence Transmission. *Telephony,* Oct. 1901, *2* (4), 168; Julian Hawthorne. A Twentieth Century Forecast. *Bookman's Magazine,* Sept. 1903, *2*, 307–312.

[10] Adrienne Yanekian. *The Telephone Pioneers of America, 1911–1961.* New York; Telephone Pioneers of America, 1961, p. 76 reports a humorous skit put on by some early telephonists in 1913 portraying communication in 2113, by which time thought transference had replaced other means of communication.

III

Conclusion

Some general conclusions about the field of technology assessment can be drawn from the inventory above, but one warning must be stated. Our conclusions derive from a particular case study of the telephone. The technology we have studied was that of a consumer product that entered into use through the market. The conclusions we draw might not apply to a new military device or to the space program, for example. The mechanisms by which such non-market technologies are adopted and affect society could be quite different.

In the telephone's case a variety of alternative technologies were available to meet human needs for rapid remote communication. The choice among the technological alternatives and decisions about just what services to offer, and in which ways they should function, was generally determined by an economic-technical set of considerations. There were technical parameters as to what was possible, but almost always several alternatives were within the range of physical possibility. What actually emerged was determined by what could be effectively marketed, for what activities capital could be raised, and what arrangements would allow for efficient billing—in short, by economic considerations.

In the list of 186 impacts that we have discussed above 143 fit that model. The 43 others in which economic considerations were not dominant were largely side-effects of the service that came to be offered—such as a decline in emphasis on handwriting in the schools or a gain in sense of security. In a causal model these would be second step results arising from the structure of services that stemmed directly from economic–technical calculations.

For a technology assessment (at least one dealing with this kind of technology) one needs first to bring to bear a technical-economic analysis that

155

explores the investment and marketing possibilities of each technical alternative. The best forecasts made about the telephone arose from just such analyses by people who both understood the technology and sought to assess how to implement it in a way that would pay. Some of the very best forecasts were made by people like Graham Bell and Theodore Vail, who not only understood the technology well but also had to face up to hard market facts on which their success depended.

Name Index

Subject Index